KUNDALINI ENERGY
and
CHRISTIAN SPIRITUALITY

KUNDALINI ENERGY
and
CHRISTIAN SPIRITUALITY

A Pathway to Growth and Healing

PHILIP ST. ROMAIN

CROSSROAD • NEW YORK

1995

The Crossroad Publishing Company
370 Lexington Avenue, New York, NY 10017

Printed in the United States of America
Typesetting output: TEXSource, Houston

Library of Congress Cataloging-in-Publication Data

St. Romain, Philip A.
    Kundalini energy and Christian spirituality : a pathway to growth and healing / by Philip St. Romain.
      p. cm.
    Includes bibliographical references.
    ISBN 0-8245-1062-3 (pbk.)
      1. Kuṇḍalinī. 2. Christianity and yoga. 3. Spirituality.
I. Title.
BR128.Y63S77 1991
248.2—dc20   90-22217
                                             CIP

CONTENTS

FOREWORD

This book is the first description that I know of in Christian literature about the awakening of kundalini energy in a purely Christian context. Kundalini has long been known in Taoist, Hindu, and Buddhist spirituality. The fact that this complete awakening occurred in the context of a classical development of Christian prayer makes it an important contribution to East/West dialogue. Given the newness of the kundalini experience in Christian circles, however, any theological interpretation is bound to be tentative.

Reading the Christian mystics from the perspective of his own experience of kundalini energy, the author sees many examples of its working in the lives of Christian saints and mystics. Since this energy is also at work today in numerous persons who are devoting themselves to contemplative prayer, this book is an important contribution to the renewal of the Christian contemplative tradition. It will be a great consolation to those who have experienced physical symptoms arising from the awakening of kundalini in the course of their spiritual journey, even if they have not experienced it to the full extent described by the author. His compelling testimony is a powerful affirmation of the potential of every human being for higher states of consciousness.

The awakening of kundalini energy and its various stages clearly enhances our understanding of how the body takes part in the spiritual journey. Spiritual writers of our tradition have long known that the body must be carefully prepared if it is to receive the higher communications of divine grace. For example, St. John of the Cross considered bodily ecstasy a weakness that gradually subsides in the process of transformation.

With keen insight, the author raises several crucial questions that arise from his experience of the full unfolding of kundalini. Prior to the awakening of kundalini he received the Baptism in the Spirit and enjoyed the gift of tongues. While appreciating the immense value of kundalini, he sharply distinguishes it from the action of the Holy Spirit. He considers kundalini a natural evolutionary energy inherent in every human being. There is a tendency in Hindu spirituality to identify kundalini and the Holy Spirit, perhaps because the Baptism in the Spirit is not a part of the experience of the East.

Kundalini is an enormous energy for good, but like all human potentials, it could also be used for selfish motives and thus become a source of serious harm. This is probably the energy that is so attractive in cult leaders; they may well impart a spiritual experience through the transmission of kundalini in a way that we do not yet understand. Energy, however great, is only energy. It is how one uses it that counts. Thus the importance of the moral context in which kundalini is awakened. Most spiritual disciplines worldwide insist on some kind of serious discipline before techniques of awakening kundalini are communicated. In Christian tradition, the exercise of the moral virtues that quiet emotional turmoil, the service of others, and the regular practice of the stages of Christian prayer from discursive meditation to contemplation are the essential disciplines. Without such positive preparation and the passive purifications described by St. John of the Cross, kundalini could serve the purposes of the false self and be used for spiritual power plays, to the great emotional and spiritual damage of other people. Thus, for a Christian at least, it is essential that their energy be directed by the Holy Spirit. In Christian spirituality, the unfolding of the stages of prayer described by St. Teresa of Avila in the *Interior Castle* may be the fruit of the kundalini energy arising under the guidance of the Holy Spirit. Kundalini may also be an active ingredient in the Dark Nights of St. John of the Cross.

Kundalini has influenced ancient Eastern methods of medicine such as acupuncture and adyurvedic medicine. As these forms of healing become better known in the West, the question as to the exact nature of kundalini will certainly arise. All the Eastern traditions concur that this energy should not be awakened except under the guidance of a qualified teacher. Since this energy can arise through the practice of ordinary Christian prayer forms, the need of spiritual directors who are at least knowledgeable in this area is evident. The personal predicament that the author describes could be happening to other Christians in our time. Moreover, as Christian contemplation becomes better known, a number of persons who have experienced the awakening of kundalini through Eastern techniques may wish to return to their Christian roots, where their spiritual condition needs to be understood.

In order to guide persons having this experience, Christian spiritual directors may need to dialogue with Eastern teachers in order to get a fuller understanding. The importance of the "Document on the Non-Christian Religions" comes into focus here. The document states,

> the Church therefore has this exhortation for her sons [and daughters]; Prudently and lovingly through dialogue and collaboration with the followers of other religions and in witness of Christian faith and life, acknowledge, preserve and promote the spiritual and moral goods found among these men [and women] as well as the values in their society and culture. (no. 2)

This book will initiate Christians on the spiritual journey into this important but long neglected dimension of the transforming power of grace.

THOMAS KEATING
June 1990

INTRODUCTION

"You're writing on Christian spirituality and what!"

So exclaimed a friend when I showed him this manuscript.

"Well, let's just say it's on contemplation and its effects," I responded.

He thought that sounded more interesting.

Unless one has read avidly in the literature of Hinduism and New Age mysticism, a few of the terms utilized throughout this work are likely to be foreign. I realize that some readers are likely to be put off by terms such as "chakras," "astral body," and "kundalini energy," but there are no synonymous or even analogous terms to describe these experiences in the Christian contemplative literature. It is in Hinduism that the kundalini process and its spiritual significance is most clearly identified, so my occasional use of Hindu terminology is a giving of credit where it is due. For those unfamiliar with Hinduism, however, a few, brief definitions are in order.

1. *Astral Body*. This is the psycho-spiritual body in Hindu literature. It mediates between the gross body, which is material, and the causal body, which is pure spirit. Sometimes called the yogic body, it has its own energetic physiology, which roughly parallels the systems of the gross body.

2. *Chakras*. The term means "circle" in Sanskrit. These are the energy centers in the astral body, roughly corresponding to the spinal plexuses. Most texts speak of seven chakras, five of which are located along the spine; the sixth is located in the center of the forehead, and the seventh atop the head. Kundalini Yoga organizes its spiritual disciplines in reference to these chakras.

3. *Kundalini*. The term means "the curl of the hair of the beloved." It is described as a very powerful form of psycho-spiritual energy that is curled, or coiled, at the base of the spine in the first chakra. When awakened through the disciplines of yoga, this energy uncoils and moves up through the spinal canal (the sushumna nadi), piercing the chakras and eventually entering the brain. Great energy, power, and insight accompany the experience of kundalini in the brain. For many, this is a short-lived experience: after entering the brain, kundalini slowly begins falling, eventually coiling again in the first chakra. It is said that yogis have the ability to keep the kundalini current flowing up to the seventh chakra, giving them experiences of extraordinary knowledge, power, and bliss.

Since the spring of 1986, I have been experiencing various psychological and physiological phenomena such as those attributed to kundalini in the Hindu and Taoist literature. Through the years, the process has intensified, bringing many positive and painful experiences. All this has happened to me in the context of Christian, contemplative prayer.

The purpose of this book is to describe the kundalini process as experienced by a Christian. As far as I know, this is the first book of its kind, which makes it significant in terms of the relationship between Christian and Eastern mysticism. The implications of kundalini relative to physiology, psychology, and spirituality will also be discussed. I believe these reflections will be of interest to spiritual directors, pastoral counselors, contemplatives, New Age readers, and those interested in Christian-Eastern dialogue.

ACKNOWLEDGMENTS

During the course of my struggles to understand and integrate the experience of kundalini into my life as a Christian, several people have played very important roles. Quite obviously, this was not the kind of thing I could talk about with just anyone, but I am grateful that I could share these experiences with my wife, Lisa. She and my children provided an ongoing support environment that enabled me to ground my experiences in practical reality.

My correspondence with the Catholic contemplative Bernadette Roberts was also helpful. More than anyone I had ever read, she described experiences of contemplation that resonated with my own. I see the working of kundalini all throughout her journey.

My correspondence with author Jim Arraj helped me to identify the kundalini process in my experiences. This discovery did not come until the winter of 1988, when the process had almost completed its cycle. Our ongoing dialogue concerning Eastern and Christian spirituality has helped me to remain firmly rooted in my Catholic faith. It was also Jim who encouraged me to write this present work roughly along the lines in which it is organized.

Members of my support group — Rev. Walt Smith, Shirley Smith, Marchita Mauck, and Rev. Bob Marcel — were most puzzled when I first took a risk and shared my experiences during the spring of 1988. Nevertheless, they validated the good consequences they were observing and provided another helpful grounding in reality.

The small group meeting for daily Mass at St. George Parish has also been important to me — even though we do not say much to each other. Simply being with others for Eucharist has been a key to integrating kundalini.

Tom Abel, my spiritual director and soul friend, has provided helpful feedback, confrontation, support, and encouragement. Also a family man, Tom is open to the working of the Spirit in many wonderful ways that have blessed me in my relationship with him.

After writing the first draft of this manuscript, I sent copies to Rev. Thomas Keating, O.C.S.O., Lee Sannella, M.D., Gene Kieffer (of the Kundalini Research Foundation), Sr. Fara Impastato, O.P., Michael Washburn, Ph.D., Bernadette Roberts, Jim Arraj, Mike Milner, Monica Freeman, and Mary Carmen Rose. All these people have either scholastic and/or personal experience and competence in discussing prayer, mysticism, and transpersonal experience. Their feedback has been of enormous help in strengthening many sections of this work. My ongoing dialogue with these people has also helped me to better integrate the kundalini experience.

— *Chapter 1* —

THE BRIGHT NIGHT OF KUNDALINI

Before the spring of 1988, I knew nothing about kundalini energy. Looking back on the journey I will describe, however, I see now that I came under the influence of kundalini energy as far back as April 1986, when my prayer life began to change in a most dramatic manner. Through the remainder of that year and up to the present time kundalini energy has figured significantly in my psychological, spiritual, and even physiological growth. The purpose of this chapter is to describe my experiences of kundalini energy and how my life was affected by this most unexpected phenomenon. Later chapters will attempt to discuss the physiological, psychological, spiritual, and theological significance of these experiences.

— Personal Background and Contexts —

Although this work is not intended as a spiritual autobiography, I believe that it is nonetheless important to acquaint the reader with the type of life I was leading before the kundalini experiences began.

To begin, I think it significant to note that my formal academic background includes nine years of college, out of which I earned a Master of Science degree in biology. I completed all my coursework toward a Ph.D. in biology, but decided in 1977, at the age of twenty-seven, to make a career change to become a lay minister. My background in science has proven itself very helpful in understanding kundalini and its workings.

During the course of my graduate studies, I became quite involved in lay ministry. I had attended a Cursillo retreat in 1973 and followed this up in a charismatic prayer group in the Catholic Church; both experiences left me with a deep love for God. The spiritual dimension of my personhood, which had been sorely neglected for years, began to blossom and bear fruit. I found myself enjoying ministry more than nature, and I began to be increasingly disgusted with the reductionistic tendencies prevailing in the biological sciences. Most of my professors, it seemed, had no room for God in their smug, materialistic universes. But neither did many of my Christian friends accept what to me were indisputable facts of science, such as evolution and the animal side of human nature. It was a time for deep, intellectual soul-searching for me, the results of which are recorded in some of my earlier books on faith and science (especially *Faith and Doubt Today*, and *Jesus Alive in Our Lives*).

From the beginning of my young adult Christian life, I had a taste for prayer. As early as the fall of 1973, I was spending long hours in silence in different churches. I especially enjoyed going into dark churches at night; the smells and the light of the candles were most stimulating. Prayer was no great discipline for me, and I had no special technique to practice. I simply enjoyed sitting in a quiet church before the Blessed Sacrament, presenting my thoughts and feelings to God, praying in tongues (Pentecostal glossalalia, the experience of a gentle, nonintelligible murmuring of praise, welling up from the unconscious under the impulse of the Holy Spirit — see 1 Cor. 14), or just sitting and doing nothing. I was changing in many ways that I did not understand, and it seemed that these periods of silence were at the root of the changes happening to me. I began to take at least thirty minutes each morning to pray and read Scripture — a practice that I maintained without the least complaint. This love for prayer, I realize, is a special gift. Would that all people could know this.

I married in 1976 and worked as a lay campus minister until 1980, when I began a new career with the State of Louisiana as a substance abuse counselor. In 1985, I decided to leave that work to strike out on my own as a free-lance writer, counselor, and lecturer. Our two daughters were seven and five — both in school — and I had a few books in print. It seemed a good time in life to make this move, but just to be sure I was discerning correctly, I made an eight-day silent retreat to take one last look at the decision.

As generally happens, the Lord left the decision entirely up to me. I was quite nervous about leaving the security of a steady paycheck with nice benefits, but very excited about the prospect of ministering in the Church again. I had enjoyed my state job, but I had sorely missed the ministry. Helping people to grow in faith was the "work" I wanted to do — and still is, I might add. But would anyone hire me? Could I really make enough money to support my family? What if it didn't work out? What kind of work would I do next? I had options, of course, but I nonetheless had plenty of anxiety about this step into the unknown.

Following my eight-day retreat in 1985, I made a commitment to extend my morning prayer time to one hour. This was no strain for me at all, especially following the retreat, where I had taken five to six hours a day in silent prayer. Typically, during this hour, I spent a few minutes reading Scripture and reflecting on the passages, then I took about five minutes to do a variety of stretch exercises to wake up my body. The final thirty minutes of the hour was spent in the silence I had come to call resting in the Still Point. I intuitively found that place inside of me where God and I seemed to connect, and I just stayed there, sometimes speaking and listening to God in my thoughts, sometimes praising the Lord in tongues, sometimes doing nothing but breathing. Many days, at the end of this thirty minutes of silence, I was not ready to get up out of my home office and return inside. Once or twice a week, I extended this to forty-five minutes, and loved every minute of it.

Far from turning me into a privatized Christian, the effect of my prayer was to move me toward others in love. I had a wife and two children, and I did everything I could to love them well. I was very active in my parish — too active, I would now say. I was up on world affairs and involved in a variety of social justice concerns. In short: I had lots and lots of energy in those days, and I spent it writing, counseling, lecturing, and being an advocate for the oppressed. I was far from a saint, however: impatience, selfishness, and numerous attachments beset me daily.

In the fall of 1985, we discovered we were pregnant again. This was a genuine surprise — a happy one, to be sure, but also coming at a most inopportune time, considering that I was just starting out in a new direction and already anxious about money affairs. Having a baby meant that Lisa would no longer work full-time, and I had counted on her salary as a school counselor to help us make ends meet. This put more pressure on me to earn money. Stress!

This was the context of my life when, in the spring of 1986, kundalini energy began to stir within. Of course, I did not know it was kundalini at the time; I did not even identify my experiences with kundalini until the fall of 1988, when they were unmistakably clear. The birth of Paul Edmond on July 26, 1986, is a final part of this context. It seems that his birth roughly coincides with the transformation of my own being to a new, childlike state. But birth and infanthood are very painful, and so it was during the early days of my experiences of kundalini.

— The Throat Phase (March 1986–June 1986) —

It all started with a little sore throat that would not go away. My journal notes of April 3, 1986, read: "Little sore throat lingers. I've had it for at least three weeks. It causes me no fever and no other complications. Guess it is just in a bad place." But what place was that? It could not be seen, and it did not respond to aspirin or anything else. Finally, I experienced no diminution of energy because of this. I was busy building a new office outside my home and very involved with writing and other work when the weather prevented me from working outside.

A journal note of April 5 states that the sore throat hurt only when I strained my attention a certain way. It was then that I began to notice that the pain was "behind" my throat — not on the skin itself. My entry on April 13 indicates that the sore throat was still there — no better, no worse. That was the strange thing about it: it was just there! I do not know when it finally went away, but it lingered until June, at least. Two and one-half months was a long time for me to have a sore throat; I was seldom sick.

I mentioned this sore throat because, in retrospect, I believe this must have signaled the opening of what Hindus call the fifth chakra. According to the Hindus, there are seven chakras, or energy centers, roughly coinciding with the locations of nerve plexus regions along the spinal cord and into the brain. The first chakra is located at the base of the spine; the second corresponds with the lumbar plexus; the third with the sacral plexus; the fourth with the cardiac plexus; the fifth with the cervical plexus; the sixth is in the brain between the eyes, and the seventh is at the top of the brain. A plexus is, to be sure, a location where energy in the nervous system comes together. Opening a chakra signifies the beginning of a freer flow of energy through the plexus areas. There are also psychological and spiritual implications to opening a chakra.

It was at this time that I began to experience a change in the depth of my prayer. Shortly into the quiet period of my morning hour of prayer, I began to experience myself falling into a semitrance state. My breathing would taper off to almost nothing, and thinking would practically disappear. It was comfortable and peaceful in this state, but there was no sense of God's presence in it at all — at least not in the manner in which I had experienced God in the past. Sometimes my breathing would come to a complete stop for a minute or so, and the visual background with my eyes closed would become a beautiful shade of blue. It was pleasant to gaze into the blue; my mind would become completely clear when I would do so. Occasionally, I noticed vague smudges of gold light swirling in the blue, and this gave me great joy. When I would "come to myself " and realize what I was doing, the gold lights would disappear, but it was easy to get back into the blue.

It was also during this time period that I began to awaken during the night, sensing a call to pray. I would sit with my Bible, but the words did not make much of an impression. From this time on, mental prayer (discursive meditation) began to be increasingly unproductive for me. And so, in the early hours of the morning, I would sit, breathing and gazing into the blue, and experiencing great wonder about this new change.

Outside of prayer, the only changes that carried over into my everyday life were an increase in my experience of energy — I did not tire as easily — and a sense of becoming more whole. "I'm changing — much less ponderous and egotistical, much more self-assured, less passionately devoted to getting things my way, and less feeling, too, which is the strangest part" (journal note, April 19, 1986). By May 1, however, I was beginning to experience a sense of emotionally fading in and out. "Sometimes I feel as though I do not know myself at all," I noted. This is a strong statement coming from a man who for years had felt emotionally stable.

I told no one of my experiences at that time. In view of the process of transformation that they were signaling, it is strange that I should not have known that I was moving into a new time in life. Part of the reason for this, of course, is that I knew absolutely nothing about chakras or kundalini energy. The primary reason for my silence, however, is that I was not at all bothered by what was happening. In general, it seemed to be very good: deeper passivity to the Spirit in prayer, more energy and less compulsion in daily living.

On June 25, 1986, I had a vision before falling asleep of the sun shining through the branches of a forest. It was about this time that I noticed that the sore throat had been gone for a few weeks. The process of transformation has been a continuum of changes, of course, and so delineating phases is an artificial business, at best. But it seems, in retrospect, that the simple vision of the sun was announcing the beginning of a next phase — one that featured my first encounters with kundalini energy.

— Lights! (July 1986–June 1987) —

Then came the lights!

The gold swirls that I had noted on occasion began to intensify, forming themselves into patterns that both intrigued and captivated me. With my eyes closed in deep silence, I was treated daily to an aurora borealis of ultra-purple and shimmering gold lights. Sometimes the lights would assume round patterns: small circles would expand and eventually dissipate, only to be followed by other small circles of light. By September, I was observing what I called the "shimmering mandala," an extraordinary circle of gold light, bounded by a trim of black, pulsating against a deep violet background. There were always four or five of these; as soon as one would fade, another would appear, even brighter and more intense. In gazing at these circles, as I did for months, my abdominal region seemed to glow with joy. It was as though I was bathed in light from head to toe, and the sweetness of spirit that accompanied these experiences cannot be properly conveyed.

It often happened in those days that, while gazing into the brilliance of the shimmering mandala, I experienced myself disappearing completely into the moment. Initially, I would be aware of myself as an "I" gazing into the mandala; then there would be no "I," only gazing; then there would be no gazing and no breathing — only the mandala. After a few seconds, however, I would return to myself, wondering where "I" had gone. For the first time in my life, I began to wonder *what* "I" was. As soon as this reflective thinking would begin, the golden lights would fade into swirls, and the visual background would change from bright violet to light blue. Nevertheless, I found that I could let go of the reflective thinking and, within a few moments, be melting again into the shimmering mandala, exulting in its magnificence.

I began to look forward to daily prayer! What new experiences awaited me? Would the shimmering mandala appear? As the reader can clearly see, it was not in my power to consciously manufacture these experiences. They came through complete passivity and only after I had been in the silence for awhile. Sometimes, the lights began to appear only at the end of my hour, and so I extended my prayer time to enjoy them awhile. Other days, they began almost as soon as I closed my eyes, and the time passed so quickly that I was amazed. It was not uncommon for me to sit cross-legged for forty-five minutes without moving, so deeply absorbed would I become in this prayer. Sometimes my legs would be asleep, even hurting, but I still sat.

As for my interpretations of what was going on: I simply did not know. I had a general knowledge of the Christian contemplative literature and found references to experiences of light in several places. At this time, the literature on Eastern mysticism began to appeal to me as well. In an essay by D. T. Suzuki, a Zen master, I came upon the term "zero = infinity." I associated his discussions of this with my experiences of disappearing into the moment and began to speak of reaching "point zero" in my journals. About this time, I got a brochure from a local Catholic retreat house, advertising a Zen retreat for the summer of 1987. I signed up at once!

There was much about Zen that did not seem to fit my experiences, however. For example, there is little in Zen about experiencing lights. If I had turned to the Hindu literature, I would have found many discussions of light in association with kundalini energy. But, alas, I was not destined to make these discoveries until much later. My own interpretation was that I had somehow developed the ability to see the changing brain wave patterns resulting from my periods of silence. As a biologist, I knew that it was not the eyes that see, but the optic lobes; the eyes bring sensate data to the optic lobes, where the image is re-created in the brain itself. That we can see things with our eyes closed was obvious to me from my own experiences with dreams and imagination. Therefore, I attached no great religious significance to the lights, except that they were another of the many natural ways in which God was ministering to me. I did not consider these lights to be God, nor even messengers of God. I did entertain the possibility that they were a kind of "visual glossalalia," a means of communicating with God outside the normal faculties of communication. But the attitude that I took toward this prayer can be seen from my journal entries, which called it "prayer of surrender." The lights came when I truly let go into God. Wasn't that what prayer was about anyway?

On a few occasions, I described my experiences to priests and nuns who were close friends and who also had experience in spiritual direction. They seemed at a loss to help me understand what was going on. This was somewhat disturbing to me, but the continuing presence of glossalalia during my quiet times reassured me that the Holy Spirit was somehow involved. It was also at this time that I began to attend Mass daily, if possible, to further reassure myself of contact with Christ. The presence of Christ in Holy Communion had long been an important part of my faith; now I found I needed Him in this way more than ever, and I felt a loss on days when I could not go to Mass.

But by our fruits we are known, of course. My attitude in daily life seemed to improve during this phase. Work was not going well, and family demands were greater than ever. I still struggled with anxiety, patience, selfishness, and numerous attachments, but not as much as in the past. There was a lightheartedness that began to emerge within that helped me to make it through the days. I took things one day at a time, and tried to live in the present as much as possible.

Perhaps the most significant fruit of this phase, however, was my writing of proverbs and poetry. I had been writing for years, and so I was quite familiar with the creative process. But during the summer of 1986, I began to experience wise sayings coming into my mind as from a higher self of some kind. Words and phrases would fall into consciousness like snow from the clouds, and I would run to write them down before I forgot them. No sooner had I written one, and another would come to me, then another — all short and to the point. This was quite different from the insights I had experienced through the years when exercising my intuitive intelligence. I had a distinct feeling of receiving messages from another, and for the first time in my life, I began to understand how some of the passages in Scripture came to be written.

I filled pages and pages in my journal, so much so that I started a notebook just to collect these sayings. Each day they came, usually in the afternoons, when I sat outside for awhile, just being present to Nature. By the end of 1986, this outpouring was diminishing, but it is hard to see how anything new could have been said by that time.

My book *Pathways to Serenity* includes a section of these proverbs and phrases in Appendix One. A few samples, listed below, are included here to give the reader an idea of the kind of writing I am talking about.

> God is my joy, ever enough.
> God is now, my joy is now.
> Love is the way, peace is the guide.
> Love now, live in the Lord.

> Get into the now of life,
>   believing you are loved by God,
>   alert for love's invitations,
> willing to let go of your way.

> If your desires conflict with the demands of reality, you had
>   better adjust, or you will be filled with resentment toward
>   the cause of the conflict.

As the reader can see, there is nothing very new in any of these sayings. For me, however, their very conciseness was itself the gift. Given my experiences of light in prayer, lightheartedness in daily living, and wisdom from on high, I began to wonder about the kind of man God was making out of me. I even began to fancy myself some kind of spiritual master.

Toward the end of spring 1987, however, the lights did not come as often. The visual background turned from purple to indigo, and the wisdom sayings had ceased. Prayer was still deep and enjoyable, but it was clear that something new was happening, and I did not know what this could be.

On April 30, 1987, I had a dream of a giant tree splitting open, gushing water from the top and branches. There was a stream nearby, and I sensed water just beneath the ground. Fish were present in all these places. "Living water!" I noted in my journal, enthusiastically. Yet little did I know about how the radiant energy of kundalini, which I had been experiencing, must also be accompanied by a change in the cerebrospinal fluid, which the dream was announcing.

— Asanas (June 1987–November 1987) —

The importance of the interpretive system in everyday life is something most people do not usually think much about. We go through our days, experiencing a variety of things, and all the while interpreting the meaning of these experiences in the light of past experiences and our ideas about how things work. As long as our interpretations of what is happening are basically favorable, we allow ourselves to be shaped by these experiences. Change the interpretation, however, and we begin to withdraw — at least emotionally — from our experiences.

Until June of 1987, I held basically positive interpretations of what was happening to me in prayer; therefore, I surrendered myself more fully into these experiences and was shaped by them into a man of improving character. With the fading of the lights and the infrequent occurrence of the shimmering mandala, it became clear that a new phase in this journey was beginning. My initial interpretation was positive: God being so good, the best must be yet to come! But how could it get better than gazing into the shimmering mandala? I would have to wait and see.

I began to find mental prayer (discursive meditation) completely unproductive, and so, in keeping with the counsels of St. John of the Cross and others, I stopped reflecting on the Scriptures during prayer. I drank my coffee, wrote a few notes in my journal, read a psalm, then moved into an hour of quiet. What began to happen was so totally unexpected that, had I known it was coming, I am not sure I would have persisted in prayer.

The best way to describe what happened during this phase is to say a spiritual "black hole" began to suck me into itself, and I could not resist. I would begin my quiet time resting in the Still Point, then the Still Point itself would become transformed into a tornado of energy, drawing me into depths I did not know I possessed. As I "fell" downward, there were fewer lights, fewer thoughts, and no feelings at all. Point zero came easily; often I simply rested on my prayer stool, breathing and sinking, deeper and deeper, too weak to resist and too serene to care. An hour of prayer seemed to pass in a second, and I began to feel the need for two additional twenty-minute periods during the day.

In early June of 1987, I attended a week-long Zen retreat, which was conducted by a Jesuit priest with vast experience in Eastern mysticism. I saw many affinities between my sitting/breathing and Zen and was eager to find out what Zen had to teach me. I had already read Thomas Merton's *Zen and the Birds of Appetite* and had relished every word. Had Christian contemplation led me to Zen? Was Zen the next step for me? I really wanted to know!

All in all, the Zen retreat was a huge disappointment to me. In comparison with what I was already experiencing, the meditation practice (zazen) that the Jesuit taught was a much more active form of prayer. I gave it a try for several days, following my breathing, counting breaths, alternating between deep and shallow breathing patterns, and so forth. The net result was a monumental headache, which was cured only when, after zazen, I would run to chapel to sit quietly before the Sacrament, passively melting into the black hole within. Zazen, it seemed at the time, had nothing to do with God, or surrender to God. The goal seemed to be to de-throne the conceptualizing Ego, and this had already taken place in me as a result of the prayer I was experiencing. Furthermore, the teachings on Eastern mysticism made it abundantly clear that Zen was about self-salvation. This was directly contrary to my own mystical philosophy, which emphasized total abandonment to Christ in the Spirit. I spoke to the Jesuit Zen master about all this, and he agreed that I should persist in the prayer that was already nourishing me. I did learn many helpful things about proper posture and breathing, however, so the week was not totally lost.

Beginning in July 1987, while sinking into the black hole, I began to feel moved to squeeze my eyes together in a most forceful manner. I also began to do other facial movements, such as looking upward with my eyes, making bizarre grimaces with my mouth, sticking out my tongue, furrowing my brow, and pulling my ears back. Sometimes, I would be moved to raise my arms, stretching them as though to reach as high as possible, grimacing and squeezing my eyes as I did so. Between July and October, I sometimes spent the whole of my prayer hour doing these kinds of things.

It was at this point that my interpretive system began to fail me, and I thought, for the first time, that I was into something that might not turn out so well. Fueling this doubt was the increasing sense of not being myself at all. I lost my affective memory during this period; I no longer had a sense of emotional continuity about my life. For example, I would hear a song which, in the past, generally brought memories and feelings, but now the song brought only the memories and no feelings. There were plenty of feelings about life here and now, but these no longer resonated with my past. Without an emotional memory, I lost all sense of identity and spent a great deal of time in my journal "looking for myself." But who was looking for whom? Which one was me: the one looking, or the one I was looking for?

As Providence would have it, I came upon the writings of Bernadette Roberts on no-self at this time. Although I still do not understand some of what she writes, I must nonetheless give her the credit for providing my interpretive system with enough hope to allow my experiences to continue their unfolding.

Day after day in prayer, I was sucked into the black hole, grimacing, wincing, and doing other bodily movements that I now see were spontaneous asanas, or yogic postures. In preparing to write this chapter, I identified at least fifteen asanas that I was moved to do during this phase. I still knew nothing about kundalini energy; if I had, I would have known that spontaneous asanas often accompany the awakening of kundalini, and the purpose of Hatha Yoga is to have prepared the body to endure these strange contortions when they come. My body endured, although there were times when I thought I would burst my eyeballs, so hard was I squeezing them.

If I had read this account years ago, I would have wondered what possessed such a person to keep going, despite such bizarre occurrences. The only response I can give is that there has been, from the first, a sense of being prodded from within to endure. While grimacing and squeezing my eyes, for example, my intellect was perfectly free, and I would ask: "Is this prayer, Lord?" Somewhere inside me I would sense a reassurance that I was really okay, and to keep going. Since my face seemed no worse for wear after the asanas, and because I could not resist them at any rate, there was nothing to do but to go with the reassurance and hope this would not go on forever.

Sure enough, by the end of the fall of 1987, things began to change. The asanas began to taper off in frequency and intensity, and my prayer was spent mostly resting in silence. Glossalalia still came and went, and purple and gold lights began to return, but only as gentle swirls. The biggest change in prayer, however, was the permanent loss of the Still Point. I can see now that the black hole experience was really an explosion of the Still Point. There was no place inside of me that I could call myself, and no emotional memory to help me find my way around. I began to write in my journal about Ego-transcendence, or the cosmic Ego, but it was to be months before I could appreciate the full impact of what had happened during this phase.

This phase also marks the loss of the *angst*, or existential fear. I had, through the years, frequently been plagued by undercurrents of fear and anxiety, but now these were gone. I could not believe this at first; I kept waiting for them to return. But here we are, almost two years later, and there is still no existential anxiety. I occasionally experience feelings of fear, of course, but they are situational, and quickly pass away. This one fruit — living without anxiety — was worth all the contortions and suffering that had taken place. It is the fruit that made it possible for many other changes to begin to take shape. I considered this fruit a sign that the deepest surrenders had finally taken place, for "perfect love casts out all fear" (1 John 4:18). A new kind of relationship with God had begun, but first there were other adjustments that needed to be made in the brain.

— Crown Phase (November 1987–August 1988) —

From the beginning of this journey until the Emergent phase in March of 1989, the environment in which I lived made heavy demands on my psychological and spiritual resources. When people would ask me what I was doing these days, I would say that I worked, prayed, and took care of kids. If sleeping, eating, and a minimum of time for toiletries be added, this assessment would not be far from the truth.

Beginning in August 1987, I began doing more counseling with a local substance abuse treatment center. I enjoyed the work very much, but found it very taxing. Coming home was like going from the frying pan to the fire: three children, tired wife, and loads of chores to do simply to keep up. I was also doing an occasional lecture and retreat, and, as always, dithering away on some manuscript. Prayer and writing kept me mentally sane and balanced. I must say, in retrospect, that this demanding environment, which I termed the "pressure-cooker," served very well to keep me relying on God for daily strength. Before those pressure-cooker days, I had been prone to occasional lapses of complacency. No more complacency after August 1987!

During the fall of 1987, at about the time the asanas were diminishing in intensity, I began to experience in prayer a prickly sensation on the top of my head. It felt like a mild electrical shock — not pleasant, but not painful either. This prickly pain seemed to clear my head of all pain and preoccupation, leaving me in a state of clarity and restfulness. I thanked God for this unusual blessing, and discovered that by grimacing a certain way, I could induce the prickly pain all day long. What a sensation it was, day after day, to be facilitating group therapy and maintaining myself in a state of crystal clarity by inducing the prickly pain! Waves of energy would spread atop my head in an area roughly corresponding to a beret, leaving me alert and empathetic with my patients. The prickly pain kept me energized and peaceful at home, too. As I said, I counted it a tremendous blessing from God.

But what was this prickly pain? Once again, I searched the Christian contemplative literature, and found nothing. St. John of the Cross wrote somewhere of fiery touches, and Bernadette Roberts's two books on no-self described all sorts of head pressures, but this was all that I could come up with. Beginning in January 1988, the prickly pain seemed to begin communing in some strange way with my abdomen, and I knew I was out of the Christian contemplative framework, for sure.

The crown-abdomen communication went on for months, increasing in intensity toward the summer of 1988. During prayer, my stomach would tighten, my breathing would all but cease, and a center on top of my head, from which the prickly pain emanated, seemed to be sinking roots to relieve the abdominal area of its stresses. I would kneel, riveted to my stool, my intellectual self amazed at this turn of events, observing this unmistakable dialogue between abdomen and crown. Then something would give way in the abdomen, the crown would fizzle with energy, and a delicious sigh would issue from the abdomen. Day after day this went on, with only intermittent episodes of glossalalia reassuring me of the Spirit's presence.

Between December 1987 through May 1988, I was awakened almost every night to take time for prayer. Sometimes I knelt for one or two hours, with abdomen and crown communing, feeling peaceful enough, but not understanding a thing about it. Occasionally, I wept copiously, cool tears of refreshment and healing, but I did not know why I wept. There were no images, memories, or symbols of any kind associated with this weeping. It then began to occur to me that my body was eliminating stress and emotional pain without my having to go through the agony of remembering and talking about the troubles of my life (as we counselors encouraged our patients to do!). I always felt better after the weeping spells, and never missed the sleep lost from the time spent in prayer.

While my pressure-cooker environment pushed me harder each day toward my limits, the kundalini communion of crown and abdomen served to keep me free from all build-up of stress. I get a picture now of this combination pushing and squeezing me, wringing out all emotional pain from my body. The Asana stage had broken the hold of fear; now there was an elimination of resentment, guilt, shame, loneliness — all sorts of emotions that I could no longer find within no matter how hard I looked.

The consequence of this wringing-out was a sense of having no body at all. No matter how difficult my days, it seemed that the body never tired. I fed it, exercised it, and rested it responsibly. But once freed from emotional pain, the body became an entirely different experience. It was like a sponge that had been wrung dry — light as a feather, and healthier than ever. Since the kundalini process began, I have been sick only once, and that was a mild case of food poisoning.

Psychologically, I was very confused. Once the body was freed from all emotional pain, it seemed that my Ego evaporated completely. There was an "I" of sorts, and I had all my memories — but no feelings attached to those memories. Furthermore, it seemed that my self awareness had become split from my self-concept. The result was that I had no idea whatsoever who I was, but I was still okay. Whatever had happened, it was clear that I could still manage my daily affairs quite well without a self or Ego or whatever it was I had lost. In fact, it was rather pleasant simply to be in the now, doing what needed to be done, letting the past rest, and opening to the future in trust and hope.

In this new psychological state, my relationship with God became more nondualistic. I did not believe I was God, of course, but it simply did not feel comfortable to relate to God as object. Without a definite sense of "I," the I-Thou relationship breaks down. So, while I knew for certain that I was not God, I nonetheless sensed that I was somehow in God, and God in me, and that speaking to God as other would only put distance between us. I picked up a line from Anthony de Mello, in which he describes the Soul as not-one, not-two. This made sense! I was not separate from God (not-two), but neither was I God (not-one). God and I were Vine and branch; I could not tell where the life of the Vine and the life of the branch separated.

All of this intrigued me to no end. Who was I? I realized that I was not my thoughts, not my feelings, not my memory, not my body, not even all of them together! What, then, was an "I"? While pondering this question one day while driving to New Orleans, I sensed a response coming from my intuitive higher self. "Philip St. Romain is dead!" came the word. "Quit trying to find him."

Somehow I knew that this was true. Except for my body and my disaffected memory, there was nothing left to the person once called Philip St. Romain. There was peace in this insight, but a million questions as well. I yearned for a spiritual director with whom to discuss these matters, but I was never destined to find anyone (I tried several times). Bernadette Roberts had written to me that the contemplative must journey alone, and so it was for me. I am not sure, at any rate, that I would have told anyone at that time that I was "dead."

By the end of May 1988, the nightly weeping episodes were tapering off, and I felt better than I had ever felt in my life. This respite was to be short, for a change began to take place in the crown area. The sweet, prickly pain began to feel heavy and oppressive at times, and I did not know why. By July, it felt as though a dagger had been thrust into the top of my skull in the center. The communion between the crown and the abdomen was finished, but what an unhappy ending it was proving itself to be.

In addition to the twisting dagger, which I experienced daily, there was also a sense of a crab-like pressure in the center of my brain. I did not even bother to search the Christian contemplative literature for validation; I knew there was nothing. For the first time, the horrifying thought occurred to me that I had gotten myself into a meditation addiction of some kind, and I had used up all the endorphins, or pleasure chemicals in my brain. I had known for years that I was addicted to prayer; the retching and discomfort I experienced when I missed prayer were all too similar to the withdrawals my patients experienced when taken off their drugs. But I had thought my prayer to be a "positive" addiction because of the good fruit that came from it. Now, however, I began to suspect that even this good fruit was to come to an end under the oppressive, unrelenting assault of the dagger on the top and the crab within.

It is impossible to convey to the reader the nature of this pain. It was not simply physical, nor psychological, nor spiritual; it did not respond to aspirin, only to prayer. It was always there, and it was total! I did my work, all the while hoping that my head would one day clear. Other people around me seemed so happy, going about their daily business, not a pain in their heads. I envied them! A picture of a lawyer on a billboard seemed particularly annoying. His face seemed clear, calm, self-assured! I, who had once fancied myself a spiritual master, now found myself doubting that I would ever have a normal day again. Had I been given the offer, I would have accepted again all the anxiety, resentment, shame, etc. that had been lost during this phase. The prickly pain had cleansed me, but then it had sought a dreadful retribution.

I found it necessary to take more frequent and longer periods of quiet. Fortunately, there was not much work in the summer of 1988, so I spent four to five hours a day on my knees, relaxing my brain to ease the pain of the twisting dagger. Following prayer, I tried to do my usual work, but found it difficult to concentrate on any task without aggravating the dagger. It was here that the short, wisdom phrases from 1986 proved helpful; they helped me to retain a perspective when other forms of thinking were too painful. There was nothing to do but ride it out. Bernadette Roberts had been through something like this; once again, I took courage from her writings.

For all the pain and discomfort in my brain, my intellectual awareness was completely unaffected by this. Therefore, I began to study the pain, to learn what made it worsen, and to search for remedies to relieve it. Out of this study came a list of self-restrictions, including alcohol, television, ambitious thinking, negative thinking, competitive indulgence, intellectual concentration, lustful desires, emotional music, and reading of all kinds. If I avoided these things, the dagger and crab did not hurt. But how to give up all these things? I loved reading, writing, St. Louis Cardinals baseball, classical music, sex, cold beer, and good movies! I did the best I could to cut back in all these areas, but I inevitably failed in one of them, causing the dagger to twist, and leading me to episodes of self-castigation, which only hurt my head more!

I tried everything to "manage" my head pains, even going so far as taking up Zen again. Interestingly, Zen seemed to help, probably because it diminished the amount of intellectual thinking I was doing. In the end, however, there was nothing to do but surrender. My journal entry of August 20, 1988, described these head pains as taskmasters, determined to make me pay a harsh penalty for any indiscretions that caused my being to contract the wrong way. This Crown phase convinced me beyond a shadow of a doubt that the brain itself is capable of movement in the skull. I could palpate the area atop my skull by wincing and thereby affect the state of the entire brain. What was needed now was complete relaxation, for the crown area was afire with pain, and the crab within was pulsating with pressure.

Toward the end of August, I dreamed of a little golden-haired boy — me! — riding in a pickup truck with my parents, en route to visit my grandparents. I was so filled with joy I could hardly stand it, so I wept for hours that night. It seemed that God was everywhere the golden-boy looked — in his parents, the truck, the clouds, the breeze, the house in the distance. The memory of this dream was with me for days. I now see it as perhaps my earliest experience of self-consciousness.

Following this dream, the dagger and crab did not seem as oppressive. But they were definitely still there, and I did not trust them one bit to let me live my old life without grave consequences. I gave up almost everything that hurt me — a wise choice, to be sure — and continued to avail myself of daily Eucharist, where I knew with certainty that Christ was present. It occurred to me once or twice that death alone might bring relief to my situation, but, needless to say, I did not indulge this meditation.

On August 30, I read an article on vipassana meditation in

"Fellowship of Prayer." The article encouraged one simply to look with acceptance at the activities within the mind, disempowering them with this loving awareness. "Why not try it on the dagger?" I thought. It was time for my twenty-minute afternoon prayer period, so I went to my office and decided to give it a try. The dagger and crab were there, as usual, daring me to commit an indiscretion, but promising nothing positive. Nevertheless, I closed my eyes and tried to observe these pains with loving detachment.

It worked! My journal entry calls it a bliss-out, and rightly so. Almost immediately, the dagger began to break up. It seemed to be uncoiling! Round and round and round it went, dancing on the top, then moving throughout the rest of the brain, de-pressurizing the sinus cavities, cleansing the eyes. "It's like a dance," I wrote. "The Spirit leads, and I follow. How good to know that it is not addiction!" How good indeed!

A few minutes into this dance brought a change in the crab as well. I felt the crab pressure diminishing as a liquid moved to the top of my head, cooling the tissues that had been ablaze for so many days. This liquid also moved into the region around my ears, bringing refreshment and relief. My entire skull felt cold, while a blue light within continued whirling around and around. It was too good to be true! An image came to mind of a babe drinking from a large tree. That was me, all right: a golden boy, drinking greedily of living waters.

I remained in this state for forty-five minutes, and felt like an angel when I emerged. Later that night, I experienced essentially the same phenomena in prayer. To this day, there has been no return of the dagger. The seventh chakra had been opened, and its connection with the cerebrospinal fluid was established — at last. I did not, at that time, know the meaning of what had taken place. I was only glad to be free of the pains in my head.

— Adjustment Phase (September 1988–March 1989) —

It should be clear to any observant intellect that the law of life is growth and change. It is also clear that no change happens without pain "bringing up the rear." Generally, most people will avoid growth and change until it becomes too uncomfortable to stay where they are any longer. It has been no different in my case.

After the blessed relief experienced on August 30, there was no more twisting dagger. In fact, for a few days, at least, I felt normal: serene, whole, and without pains or pressures in my head. I continued with my hour of morning prayer and my two twenty-minute periods during the day, but aside from the inevitable blue lights and glossalalia, there was nothing peculiar going on. Perhaps, I thought, my nervous system has finally attained a new level of stability.

By late September, however, things began to change. I began to experience in prayer and throughout the day a sharp pain inward from the ear region. It felt like sharp, pointed forceps were grabbing me between the ears, and that these forceps were constantly being squeezed tighter and tighter. It hurt! In fact, it hurt even more than the twisting dagger had hurt. I did my daily duties, but the pain and the pressure were always there. "What now?" I thought, in anguish. I did not even bother to consult the literature and told no one except my wife about this pain. From previous phases, I had learned that these things had a way of eventually working themselves out, so I tried to apply what I had learned before to this stage as well.

It soon became apparent that this "auricular pain," as I called it, was aggravated when I violated the same self-restrictions imposed on me by the previous stage. Initially, I had assumed that the passing of the dagger meant the return to normalcy, and so I started reading, writing, watching television, etc.; in short, I returned to my old ways. Assuming an attitude of scientific objectivity toward my situation, I saw that the auricular pains increased when I broke these restrictions and were considerably lessened when I was moderate. Apparently, I would have to live a moral and temperate life whether I liked it or not! Indiscretions of any kind were immediately punished by the forceps, which squeezed and pushed inward driving me again and again to my knees, where I finally obtained relief after a period of quiet.

In October, I began to sense the passage of "fluid" through the region of pain. Intuitively, I surmised that the pain itself was caused by blockage to a fluid that was trying to push itself into some new area of the brain. I began to experience daily the sensation of a highly energized liquid forcing its way through the pinhole opening that was the point of the forceps, separating tissues, and seemingly boring its way toward its destination. This boring sensation was also unmistakable; it felt like an electronic dentist's drill was reaming a tunnel through my brain. The experience was both delicious and painful, and for all my confusion about this phenomenon, I had to admit to myself that my brain was definitely more alive.

As a biologist with considerable training in physiology, I knew that the "core," or ventricle, of the brain was filled with cerebrospinal fluid, and that this fluid circulated through small ducts to the outside of the brain, forming a "shock absorber" between the brain and the skull to prevent injury to the brain. From previous phases, I knew that my nervous system was going through a transformation of some kind, and so my thought at this time was that the new relationships between nerve tissues called for different patterns of cerebrospinal fluid circulation. In the light of what I learned later about kundalini energy, this insight proved to be remarkably accurate. How I intuited these things is beyond me! I can only say that, from beginning to end, I was assisted by a higher self, who taught me every step of the way how to meditate, how to relax my brain, how to breathe, all the while encouraging me to keep going.

It was during this month of October 1988 that I came across literature on chakras and kundalini energy. The source was one of those numerous catalogs of New Age books and tapes appearing in my mailbox almost daily (how had I gotten on their mailing lists?). I noted with interest the discussion of chakras as energy centers and recalled reading about this in the mid-1970s, when I had done research on Hinduism. But all the talk about sounds, colors, symbols, astral body, and the like did not appeal to me and did not resonate with my experiences.

About this time, a participant in a meditation class I was teaching gave me a book by Ram Dass to review for her. In *The Only Dance There Is*, Ram Dass discussed the chakras in a way that made more sense to me, and even talked about kundalini energy, but only in passing. My evaluation of the book was that I enjoyed reading it very much, but could not relate my experiences to it very extensively. Nevertheless, a seed of some kind had been planted.

On October 20, the fluid pushing inward through what I was calling the "auricular portals" converged with a current pushing upward through the "sinus portal," and a tremendous sense of power, energy, and warmth became centered on the forehead, right above my eyes. I recognized this as the site of the sixth chakra in the Hindu system, and, for lack of a better term, labeled it as such in my journal.

My psycho-spiritual situation in the sixth chakra was qualitatively different in many ways from other states. When energized in the sixth chakra, I felt calm, detached, aware, and charitable. My body was as light as a feather; there was little fatigue. Living in the now became effortless, and all compulsivity ceased. Prayer was deep; the nondual experience of self-in-God predominated. My perceptual faculties were clear, and I was even more in touch with my feelings. Naturally, with fruit such as this, I wanted to live in the sixth chakra all the time.

It is here that a knowledgeable spiritual director could have saved me several months of trouble, for I made a terrible mistake. I became *attached* to living in the sixth chakra, and thereby retarded the journey of the energy/fluid toward its destination in the crown, or seventh chakra. After the dagger experiences, I wanted nothing to do with the crown any longer. The sixth chakra was the place for me! By totally relaxing my brain during prayer, I found it relatively easy to come to the sixth chakra, and as soon as I realized this state, I tried to hold myself there. Because of my attachment to this state, however, my brain ceased its relaxation and "contracted." The energy/fluid fell, and the pain in the auricular and sinus portals assumed new levels of agony. This yo-yo experience went on for months, solely due to my ignorance of the ways of kundalini.

Some of the consequences of my mismanagement were quite bizarre. One night in November, I woke up to the experience of a jet of energy streaming out of a "pinhole" atop my head; I could feel my hair moving as it fizzed outward. This ventilation gave me relief, but the next morning I was back again, trying to control and manage everything. On another occasion, I awoke to experience my entire brain tingling with energy of the sort that one feels in a foot that has fallen asleep. Then there was the night I woke up, only to observe myself snoring on the pillow. "The astral body!" I thought, and immediately I came into my body.

The experience of the astral body was particularly intriguing to me. As a Christian, I had believed all along that some part of us survives the death of the body. My brief experience of the astral body convinced me now that the psychological self (as well as the spiritual core) does not die with the body. I read a few articles on astral travel, and was tempted mightily to cultivate the experience.

In the end, however, I chickened out, mostly because I didn't trust myself to avoid becoming taken in by the experience. It was also doubtful that astral travel had any contribution to make to leading a life of love, so I refused the temptation. There have been a few other brief experiences of the astral body — like the night I awoke to experience my thumb "inside" of my scrotum, massaging the testicles — but these seem to occur only during times of kundalini upheavals.

It was also during this time that I began to experience what I called automatic breathing patterns. It seemed that a superior force had taken control of my respiratory system as well. Sometimes, while driving in my truck, for example, my breathing would automatically shift into a pattern of short inhalations with long exhalations. At other times, while just going through the day, minding my own business, breathing would become deep and delicious. During prayer, there were episodes of short, rapid breathing patterns, alternating with the above. From the Hindu literature, I learned that this is called spontaneous pranayama (breathing exercises). Its purpose is to keep the body optimally oxygenated to support the activities of kundalini and to help generate the kundalini current. I have discovered that it also helps to keep the attention in the present moment — a factor that negates the generation of emotional pain, which my body could no longer hold.

The point here is that my mismanagement of kundalini was creating all sorts of consequences for me — auricular pains, psychic ventilations, astral body experiences, and spontaneous pranayama. Fortunately, Providence again led me to the help I needed through my correspondence with Jim Arraj. Jim has written books on Jung, Zen, St. John of the Cross, faith, and several other topics. I had sent him a copy of my book, *Pathways to Serenity*, and we began to exchange ideas and experiences about Christian contemplation and Eastern mysticism. In a letter to Jim on January 9, 1989, I finally told him about the experiences I had been having. I told him I was feeling energy converging in the center of the forehead, which was the location of the sixth chakra in Hindu yoga. But I was still, at that time, confused about the energy/fluid. I called it emotional energy, which was totally incorrect, for it was more of a nonemotional form of psychic energy.

Jim responded that my experiences reminded him of kundalini

energy. He gave me a list of references and urged me to caution, for people had gone mad under the influence of this energy.

I ordered some of the books he suggested and began to search the local libraries for information on kundalini energy and chakras. The Baton Rouge library had nothing to offer. But while giving a series of lectures in Orlando, Florida, in February, I went to the library and there found a book from the Theosophical Society. The author described much of what I was experiencing, but cautioned anyone from partaking of these experiences without the guidance of a guru. He all but promised insanity for the improperly initiated.

I spent a night of anxiety in Orlando, wondering if my fate was insanity. It was clear that I was in water way over my head and that I did not know how to swim. I could not blame myself, however. I had not sought these experiences; they had come during the course of prayer. I could not see where I had gone wrong! Had I not, in fact, refused every temptation to indulge my growing psychic powers?

It was during this long, agonizing night that my higher self brought me consolation again and again. The gentleness and reassurance brought by this unmistakable voice of transcendence led me to believe that it was either my guardian angel, or Christ Himself. Higher self promised to act as my guru since there was no finding any help for me in the Church. It promised to teach me to pray, to relax my brain, to grow in the experience, and to do everything that a Hindu yogi provided for the disciple.

I accepted this promise of guidance most willingly, since it had become abundantly clear that I did not know what I was doing. Through the months of February and March 1989, the kindly voice brought daily assistance in leading the kundalini energy to the sixth chakra, and then, eventually, to the crown, where it flows freely to this day. In times of trial, the guidance is always there. All that I have to do is ask for help and begin listening.

The books and literature on kundalini energy have also been helpful, teaching me that I was not in as great danger as I had feared, and that I was having a normal experience of growth that many contemplatives have known. The authors — most notably Swami Radha, Gopi Krishna, and Dr. Lee Sannella — have helped me once again to feel a part of the human race. The ongoing dialogue about kundalini and contemplation with Jim Arraj has also helped me to keep balance.

By the end of March 1989, the "knots" in my ear had been all but melted away. I was feeling great! It began to feel as though the Dark Night was finally over. But there were still lessons to learn.

— Emergence (March 1989–November 1989) —

In using the term "emergence," I do not wish to convey the impression that the kundalini process has terminated. Even as I write, I sense a shifting of pressures and energies going on in my brain, and the literature indicates that this may continue for years. By emergence, I am referring to my acceptance of the kundalini process as an impersonal force that is transforming me in ways that I cannot consciously control. It means becoming reconciled, at least, to the fact that the "old Phil" is really and truly dead, that there is to be no returning again to the immoderate lifestyle that I once "enjoyed," and that, henceforth, I cannot make any decisions for myself without the approbation of the inner adviser, whose voice speaks so clearly in times of need.

As for the changes that are taking place within me — I am a marveling witness to my own transformation. Since March 1989, there have been several developments worthy of mention at this point. The most striking has been the ability to live in point zero with the eyes open. When energized in the sixth chakra, it becomes possible for me to live in the now, without useless thinking, completely at-one-with whatever my awareness is directed toward. There is a distinct sense of an inner eye of some kind "seeing" with my two sense eyes — as though I am actually seeing with the center of my forehead instead of my eyes. In the literature, this is called "single seeing," and it is explained as the participation of a "third eye," or mystical eye, in the act of seeing. I do not know how to explain this in physiological terms except to say that the visual center of the brain, or another structure (the pineal?) is more energized.

On several occasions, I have experienced a kind of seeing "from the top," as though the eyes were seeing in unison with the crown, or seventh chakra. This quality of seeing presents the mind with a sense of everything-as-one-arising-out-of-nothingness-every-moment. It feels like everything is in a free-fall, and I am falling with it. In comparison with sixth chakra seeing, this experience is difficult to integrate into everyday life. It is difficult to focus the attention on anything in particular; the transience and oneness of life is all-pervading. Fortunately, I have not found it too difficult to "drop down" from seventh chakra seeing to sixth chakra seeing, where the attention can easily be focused on the task at hand.

The spiritual significance of these various modes of seeing have been very important. Before sixth chakra seeing became a reality, my awareness seemed to be housed in the intellect. No matter how hard I tried, I could not "just-look," or "just-be" without thinking, analyzing, and judging what it was I was perceiving. Consequently, I was always one thought away from perfect silence — and I knew it. When energized in the sixth chakra, however, it seems that my awareness breaks free from the intellect and so is able simply to experience reality through the senses without judging, analyzing, or thinking. It becomes possible to just-look, and to see things as they are without distorting them through an interpretive filter. Sitting and looking at a leaf, or a tree, or listening to a bird becomes a powerful religious experience; it is as though I am seeing everything for the first time. The contribution of the "third eye" to this seeing is a heightened sense of awareness of the object — almost as though the "third eye" is a film projector illuminating everything with a new quality of brilliance. On one level, nothing is different; everything still has its familiar shapes, colors, smells, sounds, etc. And yet there is no denying the fact that everything seems new, special — a center of God's presence. This latter perception is a contribution of faith to this new seeing, opening my heart to the fact that God is the center of everything. Intellectually, I always knew this; now I can see that it is true.

But if God is the center of everything, it is also true that God is the circumference of no-thing. Such is the conclusion reached through faith in seventh chakra seeing. In seventh chakra awareness, there is a sense of God as unbounded mystery and of creation arising out of no-thingness in each second, solely by the will of God. This awareness leads to a profound reverence for God-as-Creator, and self-as-nothing without God, and so I count it as valuable. Nevertheless, as I have already stated, living in the seventh chakra is very difficult, and I am glad that I am not "stuck" there. All that oneness makes it difficult to manage the practical affairs of everyday living.

Happily, the Emergent phase has also brought a return to a kind of feeling self, though certainly not as of old. Since the beginning of the Asana stage, I had experienced the melting away of my affective memory. This was necessary to purge my body of emotional pain, and I am grateful daily for this tremendous blessing, which alone has made the journey worthwhile. However, the process of purgation left me with a sense of being emotionally "not there," or stunned. With the emergence of sixth chakra seeing, however, there was also a sense of re-energizing in the lower centers. But the feeling self that emerged was not the same as the one which had been lost.

The only way to describe this new feeling self is to say that the little golden boy experienced in my dreams has, in some manner, become incarnated in my waking state. Like the little golden boy in my dreams, this new feeling self senses God's presence wherever it looks. While gazing about in single-seeing, my abdominal region becomes warm with a joy so sweet and steady that I know God is everywhere and that I am in God.

My affective memory is also beginning to return, but it, too, has been changed. There is no longer any emotional pain within me and none to experience in my memory! I know this sounds incredible — even impossible! It is true, however. In fact, it seems that my body no longer has the ability to hold any emotional pain at all. I still do mismanage my consciousness several times daily, and when I do, I generate disappointment, hurt, anger, guilt — the whole mess! If I do not deal with these feelings on the spot, they will not filter down into the unconscious and the bodily tissues like they used to do. The kundalini current running ever throughout my nervous system moves these pains into my brain, where they are experienced as throbbing aches in my ear region. No emotional mismanagement is permitted in this new state of affairs — something I am still adjusting to. In the absence of emotional pain, then, the feeling tone taken in memory is precisely the feeling tone taken in the waking state by the golden boy. It seems now that the affective dimension of memory is the golden boy's perspective; I see my past in the light of God's living Providence and I recognize that everything that has ever happened to me was necessary to bring me to the point I am experiencing now.

The emergent state has also featured a change in my experience of prayer. During deep states of quiet, when resting in point zero, a pulsating white light radiates around my head, energizing the periphery of my brain. This causes a sense of heat — sometimes uncomfortably so — in the brain tissues; circulating cerebrospinal fluid brings cooling relief. Later during the day, I feel more alive —

like my brain is more awake. This has been the pattern all along: the kundalini radiant energy vitalizing brain and spinal tissues, with cerebrospinal fluid acting as a coolant and supplier of nutrients to the newly-energized cells.

Toward the end of May 1989, when the pulsating white light began to intensify, I began to feel great discomfort praying with eyes closed. The semitrance state that had accompanied prayer since the summer of 1986 disappeared just as mysteriously as it had appeared three years earlier — without warning or fanfare. I continued to pray as though the semitrance were present, keeping my eyes closed and following my breathing, but the result was a monumental headache and a scratchy pain in my ears. I could not so much as sit with my eyes closed for ten minutes without experiencing excruciating pain, so I quickly learned that this phase of the process had ended. As always, pain is our best teacher, and one that kundalini has used to move me along each step of the way.

At this time, I began to sense a call to be with God outdoors, with eyes open and senses alert, giving praise in harmony with creation. It took me awhile to respond, but since my other way of praying was no longer working, I decided to give it a try. To my utter amazement, I discovered that my body went through the kundalini process even as I sat outside, simply being present to God-in-Nature. My breathing patterns changed, the energy rose, the cerebrospinal fluid intensified circulation, and I felt cleansed as I just-sat, looking and breathing, gently praising God in harmony with the sights and sounds around me. It was then that I knew that the kundalini process had completed a major phase of its ongoing work. It was also at this time that my experience of the Still Point shifted permanently from within to without.

— Regenerative Stage (November 1989 Onward) —

The first draft of this manuscript was completed in July 1989, during what I have called the Emergent phase of my experience of kundalini. As the months of waiting for publication have gone by, I have come to experience several new kundalini developments, which indicate another phase in the renewal process.

A most significant change to me has been the growing sense of a relationship between the kundalini process and sexual energy. It seems that, in some manner, excessive sexual activity has a profoundly negative effect on my experience of kundalini. The Hindu explanation is that the seminal fluids in males are reservoirs of prana, or life energy. This prana, it is held, is concentrated in the semen by the body, and then carried via the nerves into the spinal column, where it circulates in the cerebrospinal fluid, bathing the nerve tissues of the spinal cord and the brain with its energies. When the semen is ejaculated, this process is temporarily disrupted, or so goes the hypothesis. I do not know if I believe in prana, but I can say that my experience of kundalini has affected sexual activity.

My response to this has been mixed. Initially, when reading the Eastern literature, which mostly advocates celibacy, I felt very sad about this development. I was not ready for celibacy; it was not good for my marriage. Other prominent writers (e.g., Lee Sannella) said nothing about sex and kundalini, and this lacuna left me even more confused. Then there were the Tantric sexual practices, which used a sexual ritual to awaken kundalini. But awakening kundalini was not my problem: living with it was.

As many times before in this process, I decided I would just have to learn what to do by myself by paying close attention to my own intuition and the consequences of my behavior. Happily, where it has come out (at this time) is that moderation in sexual activity is not incompatible with a positive experience of kundalini. There is no longer any question of having sex for the mere purpose of physical pleasure; sex without love brings very painful consequences to the brain, for reasons that I still do not understand.

Although it is not easy for me to write about this most personal part of my life, I do so because it has become an important part of the unfolding kundalini process. Also, any who read the literature on kundalini are sure to come across the many references to the relationship between sexual fluids, kundalini energy, and prana. At this time, I do not see moderate, loving sexual activity to be an obstacle to kundalini. One must be very, very careful in this area, however. Whether or not the prana-sex fluids hypothesis is true cannot be determined at this time, but there is certainly no doubt that willful activity of any kind will make problems for one with kundalini. Needless to say, sexuality is an area where willfulness and immoderation abound.

Most mercifully the Regenerative stage has also brought a breaking up of the energy blocks in my ears. From September 1988 to December 1989, I continually experienced pressure in the ear regions. There were times when the kundalini energy broke through these areas, flowing sweetly to the brow area. But the least little indiscretion brought a return to pains in the ear region — especially my right ear. This pain cannot be described. I was able to function while enduring it, but there was not a second that I was unaware of it. Every now and then, kundalini would break through, and the pressure in the ears would diminish. These were sweet times. I learned everything I could by paying attention to what caused the ears to block, and what brought release.

The most significant correlations with auricular pain have been angry, negative thinking and intensive intellectual activity. I have also noticed that when the ears are hurting, the throat often hurts, too. It seems as though anger and intellectual activity cause psychic energy to intensify (or coil) in the throat and ears. When we consider that thinking is really mental speaking (i.e., of the throat) and listening (i.e., of the ears), and that thinking does involve the speech and hearing centers of the brain, then it becomes clear that excessive thinking overworks the speech and hearing centers of the brain. When the kundalini current encounters these congested centers, there is resistance to the energy. This causes intense heat, which discourages thought, allowing the energy to eventually pass through in its journey to the top of the head.

As with sexuality, I must still be very careful about reading. Too much useless conceptualization causes pain in the ears. But too much conceptualization about things never did me much good anyway, so I have curbed my reading considerably with no great loss to my enjoyment of life.

The sensual spirituality that began to emerge earlier has also continued. I am able, now, to use my senses without thinking. It is a wonderfully mysterious thing to just-look and to see with the eyes without thinking about what one sees. Amazingly, there is no loss of intelligence in this seeing. It is as though the intelligence once maintained in the rational intellect has become diffused into the senses, so that seeing is not mere animal-seeing, but intelligent, nonreflective seeing. Needless to say, I am fumbling for words here. The experience of sensual intelligence is difficult to describe.

There has also been a change in the "see-er." The Emergent stage brought a return to the feeling self, which followed the cleansing of the body from emotional pain. Since then, the Egoic pole of

THE BRIGHT NIGHT OF KUNDALINI

consciousness has returned, only not as before. For although there is, with me, a very definite sense of "I," this "I" is not the old mental-conceptual Ego. Now, the "I" is just an "I." It is not, as in days of old, "I am." There is no separation between the "I" and its Ground, or "Am." The "I" is me, and the "Am" is Dynamic Ground, or Soul. Consequently, I have become increasingly aware of my attending self, or "I," as pure attention itself. It often feels like the Ground Itself sees out of my senses, and when this happens, attention is realized at its Root. During these times, there is not even awareness of an "I" that is seeing. There is just the seeing — a very ordinary experience, but very rich.

Finally, this new phase has brought a growing sense of myself as two bodies. There is still the physical body with it all it needs. Now, too, there is an energy body, which is the movement of kundalini through the nervous system of the physical body. My earlier experiences of the astral body were brief encounters with this energy body as it struggled to integrate itself with the physical body. As the process has moved along, this astral or energy body has made its peace with the physical body, from which it has sprung, and now acts in the physical body as though it were a comfortable suit of clothes.

Nevertheless, I am quite aware that the life of the physical body is one thing and the life of the energy body is another. The energy body is patterned on the physical and was given birth by it, but it now lives on an energy Source that transcends the physical. The two bodies affect one another, to be sure; the many experiences of pain I have described attest to this. But now it seems that the energy body has primacy, and that "I" am of the energy body. The physical body must be cared for, to be sure, but mostly to avoid conflicting with the laws that govern the activity of the energy body.

Quite naturally, I wonder if this energy body is not a glimpse of the resurrected state. Sometimes it seems to me that this physical body is merely a seed, from which, if all goes well, the energy body will sprout. In other words, the physical body is a womb for the energy body. Later, perhaps, in the fully resurrected state, another physical body will be given, but this time to serve the purposes of the energy or spiritual body.

Well, I am sure that many readers will think that this is all very far-out, and I quite agree! Nevertheless, it is also very real, and, I believe, within the grasp of every human being who is willing to open him- or herself to the working of the Spirit. Human nature is most mysterious, if we can drop our attachment to the familiar. But that's not easy, of course, and that's the problem.

— Summary —

During the course of growth in prayer, I began to experience phenomena that I now understand to be associated with the kundalini process. I knew nothing about kundalini when these symptoms began in the spring of 1986; it was not until the fall of 1988 that I began to learn about chakras and kundalini energy. What is most unique about this process, in comparison to other spiritual experiences, is its holistic nature. Kundalini is an energy that is at once physiological, psychological, and spiritual.

Listed below are the symptoms of kundalini that I experienced during the six phases described in this chapter. Most of these symptoms have been discussed in this chapter, but a few were omitted at this time (to be taken up in future chapters).

1. *Throat Phase* (March 1986–June 1986)

   A. Lingering sore throat (opening of fifth chakra).

   B. Deep, semitrance state in prayer.

   C. Deep blue background and gold swirls evident during prayer.

2. *Light Phase* (June 1986–June 1987)

   A. Deep blue background and brilliant gold circles in prayer.

   B. Perception of energy moving throughout the body, popping through nerves, uncoiling in plexus areas.

   C. Very shallow breathing during prayer.

   D. Sense of emotions fading away.

   E. Increase of energy in daily living.

3. *Asana Phase* (June 1987–November 1987)

   A. Deep indigo color in prayer.

   B. Spontaneous asanas (grimaces and other body movements), mostly in the face and eyes, during prayer.

    C. Sense of falling into a psychic "black hole." Very deep, passive contemplation.

    D. No colors in prayer; mostly black visual background.

    E. Loss of emotional memory.

4. *Crown Phase* (November 1987–August 1988)

    A. Prickly pain atop head, descending along facial area.

    B. Release of emotional energy through episodes of crying.

    C. Loss of a sense of having a body.

    D. Loss of all sense of self.

    E. Extreme discomfort without quiet times (kundalini headaches). Compulsion to meditate for hours each day.

    F. Sense of pain and pressure inside of head.

    G. Deep, spell-binding, ultraviolet visual background in prayer.

5. *Adjustment Stage* (September 1988–March 1989)

    A. Painful pressure in ears, pushing inward.

    B. Feelings of heat and cold alternating on head and in different parts of the body.

    C. Sense of energy/fluid coming together in center of forehead. Deep sense of peace, power, and awareness in this state.

    D. Spontaneous pranayama (breathing exercises).

    E. Experiences of yogic, or astral body (e.g., astral thumb massaging testicles, energy body floating above physical body during sleep).

    F. Inability to tolerate emotional pain in the body without extreme discomfort.

6. *Emergence* (March 1989–November 1989).

    A. Freely energizing in brow and crown.

B. Single-seeing; sense of a third, inner eye seeing with sense eyes.

C. Return of a sense of feeling self in abdomen (signals completion of kundalini process).

D. Pulsating light around head visible during deep, meditative states.

E. Beginning of discomfort with long and frequent periods of meditation.

F. Music in the mind — more or less continual.

7. *Regenerative Stage* (November 1989–Present)

A. Sense of energy pulsating between genitals and base of the spine, and coming into the brain via the cerebrospinal fluid.

B. Uncoiling of energy knots in the ears.

C. Acute, intelligent sensuality.

D. Internal energy body living in harmony with physical body.

E. Realization of True Self, "I" (self-awareness) "Am" (Christ).

Any brief perusal of the literature on kundalini will include accounts of the symptoms listed above. When I first began to read the literature on kundalini transformation, I felt very validated. Indeed, the progression of symptoms listed above follows along almost classical lines.

From my own reading, my conversations with experienced Christian spiritual directors, and my correspondence with scholars, I have learned that the kundalini process is poorly documented among Christian contemplatives. Perhaps the reason is that few Christian contemplatives have experienced kundalini in the intense form that I have endured — if they experienced it at all; perhaps, too, they simply did not record their experiences. Certainly, if one reads between the lines, one can find kundalini at work in some of the travails and Dark Nights of the Soul undergone by Christian mystics. Therefore, the significance of this work, perhaps, lies in its potential to contribute to the dialogue between Christianity and Eastern forms of mysticism such as are promoted in what is called New Age spirituality.

But what is the meaning of kundalini? And what, precisely, is kundalini energy? What is its relationship to contemplation? Is this something that one should desire?

The purpose of this chapter was to show evidence of the kundalini process at work in my life during the past three years. In the following chapters, we shall reflect more deeply on the meaning of this experience.

— *Chapter 2* —

PSYCHOLOGY AND KUNDALINI

In beginning these reflections on the meaning of kundalini, I must preface everything that follows with the assertion that there is much more that I do not know about kundalini than I do know. Even after sifting through the rather extensive (and largely Hindu) literature on this topic, I am still left with many unanswered questions. Nevertheless, it is true that no experience can be integrated without reflection and at least some degree of understanding concerning the meaning of the experience. That is what I shall attempt to share in this and subsequent chapters.

Kundalini energy touches one simultaneously on many different levels: physiological, psychological, spiritual, and social. Therefore, it is difficult to reflect on the meaning of kundalini by focusing only on one dimension — say, physiology — while ignoring the rest. The physiological consequences of kundalini activity result in profound changes in psychological, spiritual, and social functioning; the converse is also true.

As long as we keep in mind the holistic and organic nature of kundalini, it will be appropriate to proceed with the following reflections, which focus on only one dimension at a time. It is impossible to speak about every dimension at once, although the narrative presented in chapter 1 accomplishes this to some extent.

What we need now is a closer look and a deeper analysis of the impact of kundalini on the various dimensions of human life.

In beginning these reflections on the meaning of kundalini, I have chosen to focus on the psychological dimension of the experience because it is the level that integrates the spiritual and the physiological. It is also the level with which most people are familiar.

— The Nature of the Ego —

The other day, my eleven-year-old daughter, Rita, had her hair fashioned by one of her aunts. After the job was done and her aunt was raving about how good she looked, Rita ran to the mirror and gazed at herself in silence for awhile. Despite her aunt's hard work and excitement, Rita could not accept this new look. "It's just not me!" she exclaimed. Her aunt fixed her hair as it had been before.

This little incident tells us much about psychology. When Rita stood before the mirror, she was comparing what she saw with an inner picture of herself — a self-image, or self-concept. The discrepancy between the person in the mirror and this inner self-image was too great, however. Inwardly, Rita would not "see" herself with the kind of hair-do confronting her in the mirror. Thus her objection: "It's just not me."

I am sure that most people can relate to Rita's experience. Having lived through a number of experiences, we have come to hold certain beliefs about who we are. Out of these beliefs, a certain picture of ourselves emerges. We attach ourselves to this conceptual picture, and, from this base, relate ourselves to the unconscious mind and to the outer world. This marriage between self-awareness and self-concept is what I mean when I use the word "Ego."

Ego-development has been very well studied during this century. It seems that a normal process of growth features a developmental process that will be described in general terms in the following paragraphs.

— The Mental Ego —

We all begin life without a sense of self. The reality of the infant is a moment-by-moment series of impressions and feelings. These impressions and feelings arise from the Dynamic Ground of Consciousness, with which the infant is one, and from the care of the mother, with which the infant is also one. Michael Washburn (*The Ego and the Dynamic Ground*) has called this internal and external experience of nurturing the Great Mother.

With time, we discover our own bodily independence from the Great Mother — that we can move our own bodies under our own volition. We also discover that we have feelings that the parent may not share — that, in fact, our bodily movements and feelings sometimes meet with disapproval from parents. The response of the baby is to partially separate from the parental side of the Great Mother by building a defense against Her. This defensive, separating posture is what Michael Washburn calls the act of Original Repression. The parents notice that the baby sometimes pulls away, stiffens, becomes rigid in the parent's arms. It is as though the baby is saying, "I am, and you cannot swallow me up."

Original Repression, which will be reinforced later through the oedipal stage, allows the baby to differentiate from the parent. But it also cuts the baby off from the Dynamic Ground of Consciousness, the internal dimension of the Great Mother. The defense mechanisms built to avoid being smothered by the parent also restrict the flow of energy from the Dynamic Ground. These defense mechanisms are not merely psychological in nature; they are physiological as well. We might say that the baby blocks the energy of the Ground by coiling the energy around the joints and nerve plexus areas of the body. Henceforth, the baby experiences life as "my energy."

The first Ego, then, is bodily: "I move, therefore I am." By the age of three the child also has a feeling Ego, "I feel, therefore I am." There are parental messages in memory that help the child to express this feeling energy in socially appropriate ways; these parental messages, "I should," contribute to the beginning of a self-concept.

By the age of seven, a child carries within a *felt sense of conviction* about who he or she is. This is the mythico-emotional Ego. The "I" of self-awareness is bonded to self-concept, but this self-concept has been largely derived from the way others have treated the child. The child possesses an inner image of self, but this image is largely a gift (or curse) of the environment.

With the teenage years comes the realization of new powers of abstract thinking. Teenagers begin to explore self-concept; they can reflect on themselves as objects of their own awareness. The developmental project of identity-formation is largely about forming one's own self-concept. This is the birth of the Mental-Conceptual Ego.

If all goes well (and frequently it does not), teenagers will sort through all the beliefs and images in the self-concept that were given during childhood, retaining those with which they agree, and discarding others. In the best of cases, then, the Mental Ego is rooted in a self-concept that one has forged through one's own struggles, questionings, and pain.

The Mental Ego is the Cartesian self. There are still shoulds, feelings, and other mental activities going on, but the Mental Ego is most identified with "I think." "Who thinks?" one asks. "I" do! responds the Mental Ego. There, the Mental Ego is a thinking self. But what if it stops thinking? The very thought frightens the Mental Ego, and so it seldom stops thinking. And what does it think about most? The self-concept, its prized project.

The Mental-Conceptual Ego is, then, self-awareness reflexively bonded with self-concept. Its attitude is "I am...," with "I" being self-awareness, and "am" being self-concept. Apart from self-concept, the "I" does not know who it is. But because its "am," self-concept, turns out to be something that the "I" has created, there is always the fear that one is really nothing. The attitude, "I am" is not enough for the Mental Ego. This sentence must be completed with identifications (American, Catholic, Cajun, a Tiger Fan), roles (a husband, counselor, brother), values, goals, and judgmental convictions (pretty, smart, talented, etc.). The culture provides many identifications, roles, and judgmental convictions for the Mental Ego to choose from.

This first growth stage allows the individual to differentiate from the Great Mother. It is also the way in which one learns to develop many mental powers. The home of the Mental Ego is the cerebral cortex, especially the left hemisphere. It is the Mental Ego's job to develop the many powers of the cortex — especially speech, mathematics, reasoning, and music. By developing these powers, one becomes equipped to make a home on this planet. Therefore, it is a good thing to develop the Mental Ego, and it is important that this development be nurtured and supported in a balanced manner.

A problem comes, however, when one stops here. Then, the "I" assumes that the powers of the person belong to it alone; it forgets the Ground from which it has sprung. One may also become overly identified with and defensive about self-concept, causing problems in relationships. Because our cultures do little to encourage people to go much beyond this stage, there are many today who are stuck in the Mental Ego. This is a painful place to be.

The Mental Ego is about becoming somebody. But who? This question is answered in reference to its identifications, roles, emotional judgments, values, and goals — all of which make up a mega-program for behavior called the self-concept. The Ego maintains itself in a tension between the outer world and the inner world, from which it has extricated itself through Original Repression.

Of course, no Ego is completely cut off from the unconscious. To the extent that one is open to one's feelings and emotions, one is open to the unconscious. This is not to say that the unconscious is only about feelings, but that emotions are the energy that connects the unconscious levels of the psyche to the Ego. Many people are open to their feelings, but many are not. Some people lived through emotionally difficult childhood times, and so have built a defense between the Ego and these emotions; others (especially men) were taught that it was wrong to show feelings — especially vulnerable ones. Because of repressed emotional pain and ignorance about expressing feelings, many people become locked into the Mental Ego. Such people are generally self-centered, or Ego-centric, obsessed with their identifications, roles, self-judgments, values, and goals. Because these are all self-centered, they sabotage all efforts to connect intimately with others. Not only is one cut off from the energies within, but also from the love of others as well.

People locked in the Mental Ego eventually experience despair. It may take years for this to happen, but it will happen. That is because the Mental Ego is not the True Self. But neither is it a false self, as Easterners maintain. The Mental Ego is a stage in our growth; the "I" that is attached to self-concept in the Mental Ego is the conscious, individual awareness, which is very real. To say that the Mental Ego is a false self gives the impression that the "I" is not real, which is absurd. Everyone knows that the "I" is real! If it is not, then life is a joke. What is false about the Mental Ego is that the "I" is totally identified with self-concept, which it, in fact, believes itself to be.

At the risk of going off on a tangent, I wish to share my conviction that the large numbers of people using addictive involvements (alcohol, drugs, sex, gambling, shopping, romance, food, co-dependency, work) today give testimony to the large numbers of people playing out the last energies of the Mental Ego. Finding the Ego stuffy and devoid of pleasurable energy, they turn to addictive involvements to experience a "greater power." Addiction, then, can be seen as a symptom of ecstasy-deprivation. Of course, these addictive involvements work only for awhile; eventually, they bring more emotional pain, hardening the Ego even more in a wall of defenses.

Despair seems like the end, but it is only the end of the Mental Ego. For despair helps the Ego to realize that it is not God, a very good lesson for an Ego to learn. There are many, many casualties at this point; suicides, homicides, and divorces are but three examples. But many there are who suffer through this despair to find faith in a power greater than Ego. Such faith in a Higher Power — for me, Christ — marks the beginning of a new stage of growth.

— The Spirit-Centered Ego —

With the act of faith in Christ (or another Higher Power), the Ego relinquishes its claim to be God. The defenses relax, and healing energies from the unconscious are communicated by the Holy Spirit into the Ego itself. The Spirit moves the "I" to fall in love with Christ and so begin focusing the self-concept in the teachings of the New Testament.

It is as though the doors and windows of the Ego are thrown open, allowing the old, stagnant energies to escape as the breeze of the Spirit blows through.

Of course, one does not experience the fullness of this stage of growth with the first act of faith. The dethroning of the old Mental Ego and the transformation to a new, Spirit-centered Ego takes time.

There are two movements involved here. The first is the recentering of the self-concept in Christ. One does not lose self-concept; rather, self-concept is transformed to a religious self-concept. The primary identification of the new self-concept is with Christ; its primary role is as disciple and minister; its primary self-judgment is that "God loves me"; its primary value is love; its primary goal is to build the kingdom. Through reading, discursive meditation, preaching, teaching, sharing with others, and, especially, living a life of love, the new, Christian self-image overlays and eventually displaces the old self-concept. In the journey from the old to the new, the defense system of the old Ego must be broken down to allow the New Wine of the Spirit to animate consciousness. This is, I believe, the Dark Night of the Senses that St. John of the Cross wrote about. This is painful and disorienting, but only for a short while.

The second movement in the new life is the opening to the Spirit. It is possible for people to place primary importance on building a Christian self-concept while neglecting the life of the Spirit. If this second movement is neglected, one will simply end up with a Christian Mental Ego rather than a Spirit-centered Ego. This is, alas, the fate of too many Christians today.

The opening to the Spirit takes place primarily through prayer of surrender. This may happen during daily periods of personal prayer, and also during communal prayer and worship. In prayer of surrender, one opens the Christian Ego to the energies of the Spirit that emerge from within and from the love of others. One does not abandon self-concept here, but, rather, invites the Spirit to energize the Ego and give it direction. The Pentecostal Baptism of the Holy Spirit with its various psychic gifts, especially glossalalia, establishes the Ego in a relationship with Spirit that continues throughout the day to guide the Ego in its work. Pentecostalism is not the only way to open to Spirit, but it is certainly one of the best.

When one is open to the Spirit, the Christ-center in the Christian self-concept is a living center. Christ, of course, is not merely a concept, but a Person. But Christ's presence as a Person can be experienced only when one is open to the Spirit, for the Spirit is the Life of Christ. Centered in Christ, and moved by the Spirit, the Ego becomes balanced between the extremes promoted by the world without and the unconscious within. One also experiences a partial transformation of the unconscious, such as a healing of emotional pains, which propped up the first, Mental Ego.

Centered and open, then, the Ego experiences life with more serenity. By learning to live between the extremes, it programs into memory a wide variety of loving behaviors that will later arise spontaneously after the Ego has vanished. It is the job of this Spirit-centered Ego to live in the world, working to transform the world through loving service, and, in so doing, to become a loving person. This lifestyle conflicts with many of the ways of the world, and so one must look to the community of believers for support in living the Christian life.

Just as the world supplies a culture that encourages the development of a Mental Ego, so does the Church provide a culture for the development of the Spirit-centered Ego. Furthermore, it is the mission of the Church to transform culture so that the first Mental Ego is moral, balanced, and open to transcendence. Needless to say, the Church has its work cut out.

On a final note, I believe that this stage of Ego-development is unique to Christianity. It seems to me that Eastern religions strive to form a moral Mental Ego, then to regress this Ego through meditation into the Ground. Christianity, too, will eventually regress the Ego into the Ground, but through a very different process, which first involves a remaking of the Ego itself. Far from seeing the Ego as an obstacle to salvation, Christianity makes use of the Ego through the process of transformation to save the world. (As Gerald May put it, self-image [which is of the Ego] is God's work horse. Rooted in the Ground through the Spirit, the "I" is already "Home," in one sense, when the Ego is broken open. This makes for a more peaceful transition, even though there is still disorientation.

— Regression of the Ego —

Although the Spirit-centered Ego is a great improvement over the Mental Ego, it is, nevertheless, still an Ego. It still possesses the following characteristics:

1. It is still self-awareness tied to self-concept, although the new self-concept is focused in Christ.

2. It is still willful, caught up in the energies of Original Repression, pushing itself away from the inner Ground. There is an inner civil war — a tension between God's will and "my will."

3. It is still a thinking self, finding it difficult to enjoy mental silence or sensual intelligence.

4. It is still prone to believe that its loving energies are its own, and to take credit for its good works.

5. It still believes, to some extent, that it is in control of the journey.

6. It still gets caught up in the world from time to time through old emotional programing.

7. It still wants to be somebody, only now in a religious sense. It becomes caught up in spiritual pride.

These are problems to which many religious writers have addressed themselves — myself included. In the end, however, there is absolutely nothing that can be done to completely eliminate any of these struggles, for they all inhere from the nature of Ego itself. As long as the "I" is tied to self-concept, which it has created, it will continue to be proud of itself in some manner. The only thing one can do is to continue to focus one's life in love, and to surrender oneself to the Spirit daily, ever maintaining vigilance and suspicion toward the forces of pride. This is the way it must go for awhile — maybe even a long while — and there is nothing the Ego can do to free itself from this struggle.

When the time is right — and only God knows when this moment comes — God will bring the liberation that one seeks. This will come only after the Ego has taught the brain how to live, however, for the journey that follows depends entirely upon a well-programmed brain that has learned its lessons through suffering in the service of love. Then will come the reversal of the energies of Original Repression, and the Ego will begin to experience in full the energies of the unconscious and the Ground.

The regression of the Ego happens differently for everyone. For some it happens gradually, like a leaf falling from a tree. For others, like myself, it happens like a watermelon falling off a cliff. Age plays a role here, along with one's practice of prayer and other factors. I believe, for example, that my daily experiences doing multifamily group therapy helped to activate the unconscious.

Whatever the cause, it will become apparent to the recipient that something significant is going on. Several friends shared with me that they felt like a volcano was about to explode. If one has learned to live in the Center, there will be serenity — even during times of extreme disorientation. That is why the previous growth stage is so important.

It must be said here that there are many who regress into the unconscious and do not fare very well. The psychiatric hospital where I worked gives testimony to this. Sadly, the regression of the Ego is not always effected in the service of Transcendence. Often, it is a consequence of an emotionally overloaded unconscious, which the Ego can no longer keep at a distance. I suspect, however, that quite a few psychiatric patients are budding mystics who are misdiagnosed by psychiatrists, who do not consider spiritual emergence in their diagnoses. At one point in the journey, I experienced symptoms of various personality disorders and profound dissociation, but because I did not panic, these symptoms eventually went away.

The developmental environment of the Mental Ego is the family, school, and world; for the Spirit-centered Ego, it is the Church. What, then, is the environment for those undergoing regression?

This is a problem! In the East, there are ashrams; in the West, monasteries. But what about laypeople who undergo regression in the service of transcendence? For some, perhaps, it will involve a stay in a mental hospital. For others, as I say, it is a problem!

Bernadette Roberts told me that this way must be traveled alone, and so I did. I must say, however, that my family — especially my wife — was supportive all throughout the journey. Everyone going through this period will need both privacy and the support of a few loving people. At this time in history, we are not well prepared to help people through these times.

There were for me two phases of this regression, which shall be discussed below. The first was the cleansing of all emotional pain from the body. The second is the connecting of the "I" with its Ground, or "Am." I attribute both of these phases to the action of kundalini. When I speak of kundalini, here, I am speaking of the energies of the Ground that, under the direction of the Holy Spirit, effect these transformations. On a psychological level, which is the concern of this chapter, kundalini can be defined as libido, or pure psychic energy. The pages that follow discuss my experiences of libido, or psycho-kundalini, and its effect on the Ego.

— Kundalini and the Ego —

When my experiences with kundalini began three years ago, I was on a fairly normal course of Christian growth. I had chosen a career out of internalized Christian values, and so I was operating primarily out of a Spirit-centered Ego. I was still in touch with shoulds and conventional expectations, but I had fairly well died to these dimensions during a Dark Night of the Soul I experienced in 1974–75. In the spring of 1986, then, at the age of thirty-five, I was mostly goal-oriented and self-directed. This self-direction I submitted daily to God in prayer, and so I trusted that God's will would be revealed in the virtuous spontaneities that welled up in my heart. I was aware, too, that there were unconscious energies within that needed to be integrated. But I was ready for this, having read much about it and learned through my counselor training how to deal with the unconscious when it began to assert itself. I was psychologically healthy, balanced, and self-assured.

One of the first things that happened to me, when in 1986 my prayer deepened, was a sense of having lost myself. The union between self-awareness and self-concept was dissolved, and without a self-concept mirror to gaze into, I no longer knew myself. I still had a self-concept; my beliefs and convictions about myself were still there: I could "see" them in my mind and list them in my journal. But the *emotional bond* with self-concept was severed, along with all emotional memories connected with this self-concept. Considering that Ego *is* this union between self-concept and self-awareness, what happened when this union was broken was that the Ego itself was shattered!

Without an Egoic base of any kind from which to integrate experiences, my experience of life changed completely. Intellectually, I knew something incredible had happened, but I felt absolutely no fear about it. In fact, the shattering of Ego brought the end of fear and the beginning of a nondual experience of God that has persisted to this day. Learning to understand this new psychological state of affairs did not come easily, however. For many months, I kept waiting for my old sense of self to return.

I do not recall when it happened, but there came a time when I began to wonder: "Who is looking for whom?" Who was this "I" that was looking for itself? Eventually, the "I" gave up the search for its conceptual partner and began to live a new life. This experience of "I" is what, in *Pathways to Serenity*, I called the Cosmic Ego. My friend Jim Arraj calls it the non-ego Ego, for unlike previous Ego-states, in which the "I" was experienced as *part* of the whole of oneself — a localized center of psychic activity — this new state is nonlocalized. I still have values and beliefs and must still make decisions; the only difference is that the "I" that makes the decision acts out of a much wider field of awareness than before.

— Kundalini and the Unconscious —

In attempting to understand the relationship between the kundalini process and the non-Egoic state that resulted from it, I have come to believe that a thorough transformation of the unconscious has been accomplished. No matter how hard I look, I cannot find a trace of emotional pain concerning my past! This amazes me more than anyone else, for as a therapist I am aware of how very little clinical work I did to arrive in this state. I relived very few memories, and although I cried gallons of tears, I cannot for the life of me tell you what they were about. The healing of emotional pain accomplished during the kundalini process by-passed the route of remembering, forgiving, modifying self-concept, resetting values, and all the other hard, tedious work that accompanies the usual clinical journey through the Shadow. To be sure, I had to change my conscious attitudes so that I generated no more emotional pain, but that was a priority in my spirituality anyway.

A conclusion that forces itself upon me as a consequence of the past five years is that the body itself is the bulk of the unconscious. This is not to collapse psychology into physiology, but to point out the dynamic relationship between the two. I am a believer in a hierarchical universe, in which the psychological level is qualitatively different from the physiological. Nevertheless, psychological experience is limited by physiology, as cases of genetic mental illnesses teach us all too well. On the other hand, psychological experiences affect physiology, as when the perception of danger triggers the release of adrenalin into the body.

All psychological experiences in this life take place in the body and affect the body in some manner. Psyche and body communicate through the medium of feelings. On the psychological side, thinking takes place; from the body's side, chemical reactions take place; feelings are the consequences of thoughts in a chemical body.

All through the day, we have feelings about what is happening to us. If these feelings are painful and we fail to express them appropriately, then they are stored in some manner in the body and become physiological emotions. Feelings are the psycho-physiological responses to what is happening here now; emotions are feelings that happened long ago.

A problem arises when the body is filled with emotions. A feeling in the "now" then begins to resonate with similar emotions in the body from the past, intensifying the feeling and generating compulsive reactions. We say such a person has become "emotional"; their emotional response is out of proportion to the events taking place. Chances are very good that a person in this state will not act responsibly — will, in fact, only dump more emotional pain into the body. As an addiction counselor, I have learned that many people seek addictive involvements to get relief from this sorry state of affairs by changing body chemistry to produce chemical feelings.

By learning to change habits of thinking, one can begin to diminish painful feelings about what is taking place. For example, suppose I respond to a traffic jam by thinking: "This is terrible! I'll be late for work, and I'll get a good scolding!" Impatience, anxiety, and resentment are a sure result from this thinking as the body gears itself up to meet a threat. But suppose I say: "A traffic jam! Too bad! I can't do anything about it, however, so I might as well enjoy the radio." Not as much pain will come from this response. The more nonjudgmental we can be about what is taking place, the calmer our response.

Of course, this is difficult when one has been reacting emotionally to traffic jams for years. These past emotional memories are stored in the body, and their cognitive correlates are waiting to be activated when a new traffic jam presents itself. Emotional pain biases one in the direction of selfishness before anything takes place, and overcoming this selfish bias is very difficult through positive thinking alone.

This little meditation demonstrates the profound significance of the kundalini process. By healing the body of emotional pain and dissociating the "I" from its self-concept, kundalini makes it possible to respond to life, rather than to emotionally react. If a traffic jam occurs, the old "tapes" can be heard playing, but only as a distant, background noise (after awhile, they are not heard at all).

It is as though each experience takes place for the first time, with no emotional biases to distort one's responses. In this state, feelings are still possible — more than ever! But feelings do not resonate with emotions, and so they are more enjoyable and instructive. If I repress an unpleasant feeling, the kundalini current sweeps it right up out of my tissues and brings it into the brain, where its cognitive distortions are unmasked. If I do not deal with it appropriately, I have a monstrous headache!

Once the body is cleansed of emotional pain, it feels as though the unconscious itself has been lost. In fact, it feels as though there is no longer any interiority. In such a state, it is not necessary to have an Ego that arbitrates between outer and inner reality, for there is no inner reality that needs to be attended. Ego-reflexivity breaks down completely. No longer does one compare this present experience to past experiences. The emotional aspects of the past are forgotten within seconds (unless one has generated emotional pain and repressed it, that is)! Each present moment reveals itself as new. The lessons from the past are available in helping one to respond to the needs of the present, but this response arises spontaneously, and without reflection.

— Second Childhood —

The psychological state that exists after a kundalini transformation is similar, in many respects, to the Child state. There are no unconscious emotions to distort conscious awareness, and so each moment is received fresh and new. The difference between this kundalini Child and the first Child state, however, is that a lifetime of experiences and lessons learned are available to the kundalini Child, while the first Child must be taught from "without," by parents.

I am amazed at how this adult Child "knows" what to do. Unlike previous Ego states, where decision making involved reflection on options, projections of roles, consideration of others' opinions, etc., the adult Child simply opens to the experience, and the appropriate response emerges automatically. One is still free to question this automatic response, or to go through the decision-making process as before, but one will seldom make a better response than the one selected automatically. It took me over a year to learn to trust this spontaneity. The guideline I finally set for myself was to go with whatever suggested itself spontaneously, provided it did not lead to sin. I have never regretted a single "decision" made by the adult Child.

Lest the reader misunderstand what I mean by spontaneity here, I need to say that I am not talking about living by instinct. Prior to my transformation, living by instinct would have been synonymous with living selfishly. One of the major tasks of the Ego is to check the selfish impulses emerging from the unconscious. Because these selfish impulses are largely a consequence of emotional pain, however, the elimination of emotional pain effected by kundalini allows for the emergence of new spontaneities. Therefore, I do not encourage anyone to live spontaneously or to repress Egoic stewardship over the energies of the unconscious, unless that person is completely done with emotional pain.

The adult Child, or Cosmic state, is not a mental-conceptual Ego, but the absence of Ego. Its psychic "center" is nowhere in particular and everywhere in general. Therefore, it is virtually incapable of projecting itself into other possibilities. It cannot "see" itself doing one thing or another; it can only do what needs to be done in this now-moment. The adult Child is quite capable of planning for the future, or setting goals, or projecting possibilities, but it has no emotional bond whatsoever in the future, and cannot see itself in this future. Whenever it tries to "see" itself in any way, it begins to attach again to self-concept: Ego returns, and the brain feels tight — like the head has been squeezed into a small hat.

One of the great revelations for me has been the truth of behaviorist psychology. As a therapist, my preferred methods have favored insight and cognitive restructuring approaches, and I tended to eschew behaviorism. While I by no means wish to say that behaviorism is absolute truth, I nonetheless came to see that many sophisticated behavioral repertoires can take place without the supervision of a conscious Ego. It is these behavioral repertoires that the adult Child spontaneously draws upon throughout the day, without the need for extensive reflection. Even skills as complex as facilitating a therapy group emerge un-self-consciously. Again, however, we must acknowledge that it was the work of the Ego in the earlier stages of growth to learn, modify, and preside over the mastering of these skills.

— Altered States of Consciousness? —

After reading chapter 1 of this work, a very competent spiritual director gave me positive feedback about this journey, but cautioned me against pursuing altered states of consciousness. Undoubtedly, there are many who associate the words "kundalini" or "meditation" with altered states. Therefore, a few words on this topic seem in order.

Not once during this entire journey have I experienced what I would call an altered state of consciousness! Even during the deepest, sweetest mystical experiences, or while enduring the bizarre pressures and movements of energy in my head, I have been of sound mind and judgment. Furthermore, I have not missed a single day of work nor curtailed any family involvements because of kundalini. If anything, I am likely to view my previous consciousness — with its preoccupations, projections, and anxieties — as an altered state. What I experience now feels natural, ordinary, and normal.

The few brief experiences I had of the astral body also do not qualify as altered states. I knew I was having the experiences; I was in my right mind. I do not know how to explain these experiences, except to say that it is irrefutably possible for the psycho-spiritual dimension of our being to partially dissociate from the body for brief periods. I do not consider this a special accomplishment, nor a sign of holiness, still less a desirable goal for the spiritual seeker. Those who indulge in this experience seem to become quite taken up with it; perhaps it is, for them, an altered state of some kind.

—Jungian Interpretations—

After reading chapter 1 of this work, Jim Arraj wrote to me the following:

> If my mathematics is right, the kundalini experiences started when you were about 36, which fits in very well with the Jungian perspective of the time for major upheavals of psychic energy. The dreams you record in this chapter, especially the one of the tree splitting open, are graphic portrayals of the alteration of the flow of psychic energy. I suppose it would be possible to frame an explanation — not a reductive expla-

nation! — of your experience from a Jungian point of view. It would run something like this: you reach the midpoint of life, 35 or so, and feel the need to strike out on your own. This could be connected with the diminishment of the earlier more discursive or sensible and palpable graces of conversion so that whether outside in your professional or inside in the evolution of your spiritual life you are faced with the challenge of how to go deeper and further. This means that the stage is set for an increasing decrease of energy available to the Ego. Psychic energy is draining from the Ego, and at one point you talk about the black hole. The energy that leaves consciousness and therefore affects the Ego by a growing sense of non-ego or loss of affective memory, this psychic energy is going somewhere. It is falling into the depths and setting the stage for the activation of kundalini, or from a psychological perspective, the activation of the unconscious and its contents symbolized by the water just beneath the surface and the presence of the fish. The old Philip has to die because the center of the personality is no longer the Ego.

I basically agree with this analysis. On a strictly psychological level, this interpretation seems quite true to the facts of my case. With regard to this present study, the key sentence states that "It [conscious energy] is falling into the depths and setting the stage for the activation of kundalini, or from a psychological perspective, the activation of the unconscious...." When we consider that no significant psychological change is possible without changing the physiological base out of which the psyche emerges, the relationship between my psychological transformation and the kundalini process that accompanied it becomes comprehensible. When, in addition, we consider that the body is the largest part of the unconscious, then the terms "activation of kundalini" and "activation of the unconscious" become synonymous.

It should be noted at this point, however, that modern psychologists — Jungians included — do not know much about kundalini. Lee Sannella, M.D. (*The Kundalini Experience*), is one of the few health professionals who have seriously studied this process. Jung also studied kundalini, but considered it an intriguing example of his catch-all mythos of individuation. In a seminar on kundalini in 1932, Jung noted that the awakening of kundalini has seldom been observed in the West, and that "it would take a thousand years for the kundalini to be set in motion by depth analysis." I totally concur with the latter observation, but I am not so sure about kundalini's virtual absence in the West.

One dimension of Jungian psychology that has been most helpful is the teaching concerning the four functions: intuition, sensation, thinking, and feeling. According to Jung and his followers, these are the means by which consciousness perceives and interprets reality. They also maintain that one's capacity to energize in these four functions changes through the years. Harold Grant, Ph.D., who is a good friend and a Jungian scholar, once counseled me that I would have to come to terms with my least preferred function at about the age of thirty-five. This has certainly happened! My old preferred way of energizing was unquestionably by introverting my intuition; extraverted feeling and introverted thinking were also important. However, everything from my contemplative prayer style to my writing gifts drew energy from introverting my intuitive function.

During the past three years, I have experienced a gradual diminution of my ability to energize within, and an increasing desire to energize through my senses. This was predicted by Harold Grant. Now, I find it virtually impossible to experience God within; what I called the Still Point was the union I experienced with God through the function of introverted intuition. What seems to have happened is that I have been turned "inside out": the God-Self-center (the Still Point) is no longer experienced within, but without, in everything I encounter. This is the mystical experience to be expected in extraverted sensation.

I am very impressed that Jungian psychology so accurately predicted this change in the manner in which I energize through the four functions! Knowing about this ahead of time through reading Grant's book (*From Image to Likeness*) helped me to understand this dimension of my journey. I cannot say, however, that this has been the primary work of kundalini. As we have noted several times, there are many things going on at once. The emergence of the inferior function (extraverted sensation) is one "work" that has gone on during the past three years, but it is doubtful that the awakening of kundalini was necessary to accomplish this. Many people integrate the inferior function without having to go through what I have endured. I knew this was coming, and have been taking time outside to be with God in Nature for years. Therefore, I am inclined to say that psychological factors such as those mentioned by Jim Arraj and Harold Grant contributed to the awakening of kundalini. These factors alone do not explain it, however.

— Communication Skills —

Early in the kundalini process, at about the time the proverbs were coming to me spontaneously, I became intensely concerned with human communication. I recognized that we create emotional pain according to the way we interpret reality, and we spread our dis-ease through communication. A major challenge that then presented itself was how to communicate the reality I perceived without distortion. How, especially, could I communicate my feelings and expectations without generating problems for myself and others? The result of this period of study was published in my book *Lessons in Loving*.

When, much later, I became acquainted with the literature on kundalini, I was struck by the emphasis placed on language and communication. The goddess Shakti, who *is* kundalini, is also the goddess of speech. In Kundalini Yoga, one is taught that each word spoken is spoken by the goddess herself. To distort speech in any way is to incur the wrath of the goddess, whose very power hurts the sinner through the process of distortion. On a psychological level, I have found this to be true.

I am now struck by the many references in the world's religions to right speech. In Buddhism, it is part of the Eightfold Path. The teaching of Christ tells us to avoid swearing, multiplication of words, and idle speech. The New Testament Book of James goes on at length about the power of the tongue to build up or destroy. Clearly, the power of communication is a power that needs to be brought into control in the spiritual life.

I believe that this change in my manner of communication to a direct, simple style has helped to reinforce the many other changes taking place in my life. If I had continued to communicate according to old patterns, I would have continued to reinforce the systems of consciousness that gave rise to those old patterns. A new way of being requires a new way of speaking.

Deeply impressed by this truth, I have begun to teach this simple style of communication to couples struggling in marriage. The results have been remarkable! By simply changing the manner in which they communicated about feelings and expectations, couples find a new capacity to love and respect one another. Indeed, I would go so far as to say that the quality of our relationships is largely determined by the manner in which we communicate — and not vice versa, as I had formerly believed.

— Summary —

In reflecting on the psychological dimension of my journey, I can identify four phases of growth, which I shall summarize below. These four phases can, in turn, be broken down into smaller growth stages — such as the many stages that characterize the development of the Mental Ego. These four phases are a summary of *my journey*, but they do reflect a general pattern of growth observed in many other individuals. Each person is unique, and the growth of each unfolds in a unique pattern. Nevertheless, there are developmental tasks common to every human being, and the Egoic structures that accompany this developmental unfolding are also similar for all. In describing these stages, I need to acknowledge the influence of *The Ego and the Dynamic Ground*, by Michael Washburn, who sketches a similar trajectory.

1. *From Original Embedment in the Dynamic Ground of Conscious-*
   ness to the Mental-Conceptual Ego. From "Am" to "I am my
   self-concept."

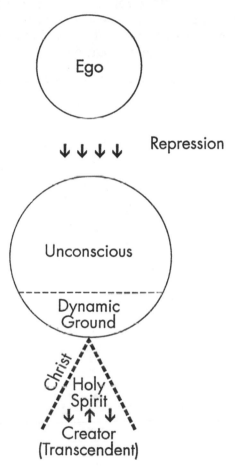

A. Through acts of Repression, the "I" of self-awareness sep-
   arates itself from the mother, the Dynamic Ground, the
   body, and precognitive energies, finally coming to rest
   in the cortex, where it identifies with the powers of the
   cortex — especially speech and thought.

B. Attitude of Mental Ego: "I think, therefore I am." Mental
   Ego is that which it thinks it is — i.e., its self-concept.

    C. Using the metaphor of self-concept as a house, we can say that the "I" of self-awareness lives in the house of self-concept, and peers out at the world through its windows. The "I" sometimes journeys out of its conceptual house during ecstatic experiences (e.g., sex, sports, creative work, movies), but its true home is in the house of self-concept, and not outside.

  2. *From Mental-Conceptual Ego to Spirit-Centered Ego.*

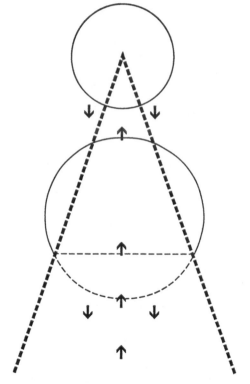

    A. From "I am myself concept" to "I am a Christian moved by the Spirit."

    B. Egoic structure is still Mental-Conceptual, self-awareness bonded with self-concept, but self-concept is centered in Christ, and the defenses have been loosened so that energies from the Spirit may enter Ego.

C. The self-conceptual house has its windows opened so that loving energies from without may flow through. Energies also enter this house from the unconscious and the Ground below. The interior of the house is arranged to give glory to Christ. The "I" is growing comfortable with the energies outside the house, since they flow through the house itself. Through natural and prayerful ecstatic experiences, the "I" is becoming accommodated to life outside the house.

3. *Regression of the Ego in the Service of Transcendence.*

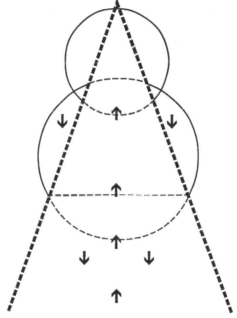

A. The forces of Original Repression are reversed as the Ego is allowed to experience its unconscious base.

B. The unconscious is healed of emotional pain, allowing the deeper energies of the Ground, or Soul, to emerge into consciousness. This energy from the Ground, or Soul Energy, is kundalini.

C. With the healing of emotional pain, the bond between the "I" of self-awareness and self-concept is broken. The

"I" feels disoriented at first, and tries to "find itself," i.e., reconnect with self-concept.

D. The Ground turns out to be more than cool, fertile dirt: it was really an inactive volcano. At this stage, the volcano becomes active. With the eruption of steam and magma, the "I" flees the house of self-concept. Henceforth, it lives in ecstasy, although at first this is experienced as dissociation.

E. Still centered in the Spirit, the "I" does not panic. The "I" does not give up its right to be; rather, it asserts its right to be. This is the meaning of the Scriptural idea of wrestling with God. Sitting in the eye of the volcano, the "I" does not move, but learns to wait patiently for the next phase, which it knows to be coming.

4. *Realization of the True Self.* "I Am."

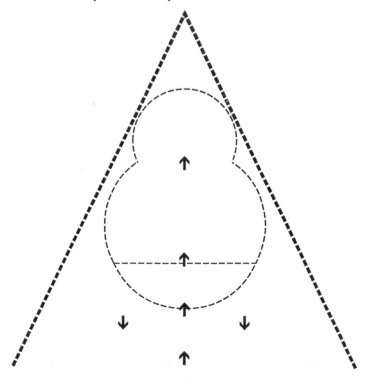

A. The "I" of self-awareness becomes integrated with the "Am" of the Dynamic Ground, or Soul.

B. The house of self-concept can be seen on the slope of the volcano, but the "I" does not live there any longer. It has found a new home for the energy it is receiving: the body. In reconnecting with the primal energies of the body, the "I" experiences itself as an energy body within the physical body.

C. There is a return to the cosmic experience of the Great Mother, as the "I" now enjoys the energies of the Dynamic Ground within, and, in place of the nurturing parent, the Cosmos without, which is one with the Ground.

D. The awareness of the "I" is experienced as arising from the Ground itself. The "I" now sees from its "Am," or root. This is the realization of the True Self.

In describing this last phase of growth, I certainly do not wish to leave the impression that one is now perfect and free of all problems. There is, unquestionably, a tremendous freedom realized when one is free from emotional pain, disattached from self-concept, and rooted firmly in the Ground. But there is no infallibility here, nor is there complete freedom from sin. One is free of the willfulness of the Egoic stages, but still subject, in many ways, to the cognitive programs for behavior learned in the Egoic stages. The Spirit-centered Egoic phase brought these behavior programs into a loving moral focus, but not perfectly so. Consequently, one cannot take one's holiness for granted, nor abandon the responsibility to make amends when necessary.

I also do not wish to leave the impression that realizing the True Self brings to end the importance of the self-concept. Even in the True Self, there is still self-concept, only the "I" of self-awareness is not attached to it. In the True Self, the "I" knows itself to be much more than its self-concept; it is rooted in the energies of the Soul, which the "I" cannot fully grasp. Nevertheless, life goes on, and one's experiences are still integrated into self-concept. Even the new, mystical experiences find their way into self-concept, thus reinforcing the cognitive dimension of the True Self.

Detachment from self-concept does not mean that one is now free to act against the moral imperatives of self-concept. To do so would still bring emotional guilt — an energy that would immediately "color" the kundalini libido with its darkness, leaving the "I" in a state of agony. In a sense, then, self-concept, although no longer on center stage, must nonetheless be "consulted" at times — especially when making important decisions. This is my experience, at least, and I do not wish to leave the impression that self-concept is no longer important when the True Self is realized.

Finally, and on an evolutionary note, we observe that there once was a time when people who grew to the Mental Egoic stage were considered oddballs in their mythico-emotional cultures. Now, however, such people are normal, as most cultures support growth to this level. Today, those who grow beyond the Mental Egoic stage are considered weird. Even in the Church, those who grow beyond the Spirit-centered Ego are very rare indeed, for, at this time in history, the Church's primary mission is still one of bringing people into the Spirit-centered Ego. When one goes beyond this, one will find little to read, and little empathy.

In biology, we have a saying, "Ontogeny recapitulates phylogeny." This means that the history of the race can be observed in the unfolding development of the organism. I believe this saying is true for those who reach the Mental and Spirit-centered Egoic stages, but not for those who go beyond. Those who go beyond are pioneers, or scouts, surveying uncharted areas.

Could it be that those who make the journey to the True Self are, in some ways, demonstrating what lies in store for the entire race? If so, then about such people we could say, "Ontogeny *predicts* phylogeny." What a magnificent world that would be — for the majority of people to be living out of the True Self state!

Such a world cannot come, however, unless hundreds of thousands of people experience the regression of the Ego in the service of transcendence, and then restructure the culture to accommodate similar growth for millions of others. I believe we are only now beginning to recognize this task. What a long, difficult road lies ahead! But, surely, there is Grace abounding to guide us on our way.

— *Chapter 3* —

THE PHYSIO-KUNDALINI

As we go about our days, we often take for granted the ordinary functions performed by our bodies. Indeed, so isolated can Egoic consciousness become from the body that we can actually believe that we are in control of our bodily functions. It is only when illness or something like kundalini comes along that we awaken to the fact that we control almost nothing.

> Young and old —
> Whoever they are —
> Their bodies are
> More fragile than the dew
> On the morning glory.

This Zen saying was brought home most forcefully to me during the past four years. Not only did it become apparent that I had no control over the activities of kundalini, but also I experienced the humiliation of hurting myself again and again by working against this power.

My biological training convinced me early on that something important was taking place in my nervous system as a result of my prayer. Experiences of light, pressures in the brain, impulses to squeeze the eyes and make ridiculous grimaces with the face, movements of fluid in the brain, tingling sensations on the skin, and sensations of heat and cold in different parts of the body all attested to a mysterious work of some kind going on in my body. The Christian literature on Dark Nights of the Soul alluded to some of these experiences, and so I did not panic and check myself into a physician's office, where I would have most assuredly been given a hideous diagnosis of some kind and a prescription of tranquilizers, which, I knew from my painful experiences with alcohol, would have only resulted in more internal upheavals. Although I had no idea as to what was occurring, I enjoyed a steady serenity about my condition; here we find one of the interfaces between the physiological and spiritual dimensions of kundalini.

It was, however, the undeniable and somewhat spectacular nature of the physiological dimension of my experiences that caused me to wonder why there was so little about it to be found in the Christian literature. To be quite frank, I learned nothing from the Christian literature to help me to understand and cope with my condition. I learned even less from Buddhist and Zen literature! Christianity, Buddhism, and Zen all provide a wealth of literature concerning the psychological, philosophical, metaphysical, theological, and sociological implications of the spiritual life. Only Hinduism, however, with its abundant literature concerning the teachings of yogis, offers comprehensive teaching concerning the role of physiology in the process of transformation. Indeed, what is most intriguing about Hatha and Kundalini Yoga is the intense focus on physiology as means to attaining profound union with God.

— Hindu Teachings on Kundalini —

As a Christian, I had never given much attention to Hinduism. I knew a little about yoga from my wife, who had studied it for a short period years before, and from those many television programs that present instruction on yoga. I knew nothing about the connection between yoga and kundalini energy, however; rather, like most people, I saw yoga as an interesting way to cultivate physical fitness. I wonder now why most yoga teachers say so little about kundalini. I wonder, too, what could happen if the kundalini process were activated in a viewer of a television program on yoga: would the teacher be available to help the student integrate this energy?

When I finally discovered the Hindu literature on kundalini, I was confronted with a teaching that moved liberally from experience to mythology to metaphysics. This is due undoubtedly to the holistic nature of kundalini. But as a Christian, I had difficulty understanding kundalini as Shakti, the inner power of God (and a female energy at that), or of the seventh chakra experience as the union of Shakti and Shiva (the consciousness of God). It was also clear to me that the chakras were suspiciously close to the spinal plexus centers. In short: I had a longing to discuss kundalini from a straightforward scientific standpoint, and the Hindu literature did not satisfy this need. I am indebted to this literature, however, for teaching me many other practical things about living with kundalini, such as the importance of the neck-lock posture.

— Science and Kundalini —

Happily, my need for a scientific discussion of kundalini was satisfied when I read *The Kundalini Experience*, by Lee Sannella, M.D. In this book, Dr. Sannella discusses his experiences with individuals struggling to integrate kundalini into their lives. Over twenty case histories are presented, many of them including individuals who were not meditators, but who experienced a somewhat spontaneous arousal of kundalini that greatly disrupted their lives. Reading through Dr. Sannella's book was, for me, what reading through the "Big Book" is for alcoholics. I felt a deep kinship with these people. It was especially heartening to read his distinctions between kundalini and psychoses. His conclusion was that the kundalini process was basically desirable, signalling a transformation to another state of consciousness that may lie on the frontiers of our evolutionary future.

But what *was* kundalini energy? This I wanted to know more than anything.

While honoring the spiritual and psychological dimensions of this phenomenon, Dr. Sannella proposed a term, the "physio-kundalini," in reference to the physiological aspects of the kundalini experience. This physiological process, he concluded, could be understood in reference to a scientific publication by Itzhak Bentov, *Micromotion of the Body as a Factor in the Development of the Nervous System*. Sannella included this paper as an appendix in his book.

Without getting into an exhaustive discussion of scientific issues, I will include here a summary from Bentov's publication, then follow with a layperson's explanation of what I think he is saying.

1. The heart-aorta system produces an oscillation of about 7 Hz in the skeleton, including the skull. The upper part of the body also has a resonant frequency of about 7 Hz.

2. The skull accelerates the brain up and down, producing acoustical plane waves reverberating through the brain at KHz frequencies.

3. These acoustical plane waves are focused by the skull onto the ventricles, thus activating and driving standing waves within the third and lateral ventricles.

4. Standing waves within the cerebral ventricles in the audio and supersonic ranges stimulate the sensory cortex mechanically, resulting eventually in a stimulus traveling in a closed loop around each hemisphere. Such a traveling stimulus may be viewed as a "current."

5. As a result of these circular currents, each hemisphere produces a pulsating magnetic field. These fields are of opposing polarities.

    This magnetic field — radiated by the head acting as an antenna — interacts with the electric and magnetic fields already in the environment. We may consider the head as simultaneously a transmitting and receiving antenna, tuned to a particular one of the several resonant frequencies of the brain. Environmental fields may thus be fed back to the brain, thereby modulating that resonant frequency. The brain will interpret this modulation as useful information.

After plowing through Hindu treatises for several weeks, I cannot tell you how satisfying it was to read the above information! Even though I do not enjoy a deep knowledge of physics, this was, to me, a healthy way to discuss physical experiences.

— The Kundalini Current —

In layperson's terms, Bentov is saying that meditation allows a standing wave of energy (sound, physical vibrations) produced by the stretching of the aorta (caused by the beating of the heart) to intensify and interact with energy currents in the brain. It is my belief that certain breathing patterns, along with mental silence and yoga stretches, cause the aortic waves to intensify and penetrate deeply into the skull. The result is a radical change in the intensity and configurations of cerebral energy patterns. One of these patterns circulates in the sensory cortex (Bentov's point #4), stimulating in sequence the parts of the cortex affecting the genitals, toes, ankles, knees, hips, trunk, shoulders, elbows, wrists, fingers, thumbs, neck, top of head, brow, eyelids, nares, lips, tongue, and larynx, after which it cycles and stimulates these areas again and again. This increases the nervous activity in these parts of the body; during the course of meditation, one can actually experience this energy rippling through these parts of the body. When we use the term physio-kundalini, then, we are speaking of the intensifying pattern of energy in the brain, and, especially, of the currents of energy coursing through the body as a result of this cerebral stimulation.

Because all nerves in the body eventually converge on the spinal cord or brain, the kundalini current in the body eventually works its way to the spinal cord. If resistance to the current is great in different parts of the body, then the current reaching the cord will be a mere trickle. Once the pockets of resistance are cleared away, however, a stronger current will enter the cord and begin rising, conducted by the cerebrospinal fluid and the cord itself. Some of this energy in the cord will find its way back to the brain, but the cervical plexus area (the fifth chakra) generally blocks most of this flow for a period of time. When, finally, the tissues (muscles of the neck and upper chest area) fed by the nerves leading to the fifth chakra have been transformed by the kundalini current, then the current can flow freely from the body through the spinal cord and back into the brain. This produces a dramatic increase in the amount of energy circulating in the brain, further stimulating, in turn, the current of energy circulating in the body.

In my own case, I now perceive that the kundalini current, already at work in my body through years of prayer and spiritual work, finally pierced through the cervical plexus in the spring of 1986, entering the brain and radically affecting my entire nervous system. It felt as though my brain and nervous system changed from a *modus operandi* of 110 volts to 220 volts. There was not a sleeping neuron to be found! I was awake, to be sure, but not always pleasantly so.

After entering the brain, however, the kundalini current still had many knots, or pockets of resistance, to convert over to its elevated frequencies. The cranial nerves in particular had to be transformed. These nerves, which govern hearing, taste, smell, and vision, put up resistance for several months. Their transformation featured the many facial asanas already discussed in chapter 1. By the winter of 1987, the current had worked through the major pockets of resistance and was then experienced as a tingling sensation on the top of the skull. My entire nervous system had been won over to the energy frequencies of kundalini. Now all that remained was for the cerebrospinal fluid to adjust its patterns of circulation to cool the awakened tissues.

— Cerebrospinal Fluid Dynamics —

Bentov mentions that a focus of one pattern of wave energy is the ventricles of the brain. It is in the ventricles that the cerebrospinal fluid is produced. From my own experience, what I believe to be happening is that the increase of stimulation to the ventricle area results in the release of more cerebrospinal fluid in the ventricles by the choroid plexus. I cannot prove this speculation with certainty; I can only say that it frequently feels like a liquid of some kind is moving around in the brain, bringing cooling relief to areas heated by the radiant kundalini current. Since cerebrospinal is the only liquid around, what else could it be?

A real problem for me, resulting entirely from ignorance, was that I did not practice the neck-lock posture in prayer — chin tucked in after the awakening. My neck was crooked, and this resulted in a "kink" in the spinal cord "house," diminishing the circulation of cerebrospinal fluid. The result was pressurized cerebrospinal fluid in the ventricles (what I called a crab), searing pain in the trigeminal nerve (ear region), and heat atop my head and on my shoulders. What I called a dagger atop the skull, twisting and turning, is a consequence of this state of affairs: the *falx cerebelli*, which is a protuberance of the skull between the two cerebral hemispheres, was experienced as a dagger. The top-center of my overheated brain rubbed constantly against the *falx cerebelli*, with inadequate cerebrospinal fluid to cushion the shock. Finally, on August 30, 1988, the subarachnoid membranes atop the brain received an adequate supply of cerebrospinal fluid, and the top of my head cooled off. I am also convinced that a new channel opened from the ventricles in the center of the brain, moving between the hemispheres, to the top, bringing added fluid to cool the brain (Hindus call this the sushumna nadi, or central canal).

I am wondrously intrigued by this interaction between the radiating patterns of nervous energy and the cerebrospinal fluid! In normal circumstances, the primary function of cerebrospinal fluid is to give the brain support and to act as a cushion between the brain and the skull; it also flows into the center of the spinal cord and between the cord and the spinal column. What intrigues me is that with the establishment of kundalini as a permanent state in the nervous system, the cerebrospinal fluid also begins to function as a coolant. It may also be carrying essential nutrients to newly sensitized brain tissues, for such nutrients can be found in the fluid. Making use of something that is already present to perform a new function is consistent with the evolution of our anatomy, however. After all, there once was a time when the Eustachian tubes were gill slits, that the ear bones were gill arches, that the phalanges were fins, etc. One can only marvel at the manner in which kundalini has re-engineered the nervous system to accomplish its work.

Of course, as I have mentioned, much of what I am saying about cerebrospinal fluid is mere conjecture. I have no proof for any of this. I can only say that the heating of the tissues and the cooling brought by the fluids is as real to me as any other bodily function. The consequences of "kinking" my neck during meditation are also very real to me.

— Sexuality Issues —

Since the fall of 1988, I have experienced a sense of electricity and bubbling of energy in the area of the genitals. The Hindu literature attributes this to the extraction of pranic (life) energy from the semen in males, and the uterine fluids in females. It is postulated that this pranic energy is carried via the nerves to the cerebrospinal fluid, where it is carried into the brain to nourish and energize brain tissues. Some texts even state that not only pranic energy, but the reproductive fluids themselves are taken into the cerebrospinal fluid. This is called the *Urdhava-reta* in Hinduism, and it is considered the mark of an illuminated or enlightened person. In order to cooperate with the body in this new state of affairs, many yogis advocate celibacy, or retention of the semen during intercourse.

There is no mistaking the fluttering of activity in the genital regions that comes with kundalini. This may be caused by the stimulation of that sensory cortical region that connects with the genitals. The genitals must surely be affected, too, by converging currents of energy sweeping up from the legs, moving toward the spine. This would not, in any way, negate the Hindu belief that prana is being extracted from the reproductive fluids; rather, this would account for the increase in energy in the genital areas, which would result in the production of more reproductive fluids and the carrying of prana into the cerebrospinal fluids. Although I am not sure, at this time, if I can accept the pranic theory, I can, with conviction, state that I do not believe that the reproductive fluids go into the spinal cord. The "plumbing" for this is just not there. Perhaps these fluids go to the brain via the lymphatic and circulatory systems.

There are many practical consequences that follow from one's interpretations of the relationship between kundalini and sexuality. At one extreme, as we have mentioned, are those yogis who believe in conserving the reproductive fluids, and so advocate celibacy. This position would be especially logical if one believed that the fluids themselves were being recycled to nourish body tissues. Gopi Krishna takes a less extreme view, maintaining that celibacy is required for one or two years early in the process, after which time moderate sexual activity is permissible. Then there are those who use Tantric, sexual rituals to transform sexual energy to higher states of consciousness. Finally, Lee Sannella and Mike Milner, who have studied kundalini from Taoist and Hindu approaches, have told me that moderate sexual activity undertaken in a spirit of love will not set back the kundalini process. This latter position has been my own experience; it is also most compatible with a Christian view of sexuality in marriage.

It will probably be quite some time before the pranic theories advocated by Gopi Krishna and others can be confirmed or refuted. If prana is as subtle an energy as they believe it to be, then it is unlikely that scientific instruments will be able to detect it. Also, if one accepts the prana-sexual fluids hypothesis as one of the essential parts of the kundalini experience, then one is also maintaining that women who have had a hysterectomy, or even those who have been through menopause, should not be able to enjoy the full kundalini experience. At this time, there are no statistics on this matter. Indeed, most of the literature on kundalini is written by men from the male's point of view. Swami Radha calls attention to this in her book *Kundalini Yoga for the West*. Again, we find that there is much more about this topic that we do not know than that we can state with dogmatic certitude.

— Inner Seeing —

One of the first consequences to be experienced following the opening of the fifth chakra is the ability to see inner light. The visual background (with the eyes closed) turns blue, and golden swirls frequently appear against this background. Swami Muktananda, a celebrated authority on kundalini, writes, "one is able to see the universe as it really is: a mass of blue light which sparkles and scintillates all the time and which is not discernible through the physical eyes." I do not know that this is the true color of the universe, but I can attest to the captivating influence of inner light.

Da Love Ananda, another authority on kundalini and spirituality, considers the perception of these inner lights to be a consequence of attention becoming centered in the brain core. In his book *Easy Death*, he discusses the significance of these different colors in relation to the ascent of consciousness. Drawing from the *Tibetan Book of the Dead* and his own experiences, he provides an in-depth discussion of the different colors of light in relation to what he calls the Cosmic Mandala. The red colors are associated with gross, emotional identifications; golden-yellow with the lower astral regions; dark blue/black as transitional between the higher astral regions and the subtle realms; brilliant blue with the subtle planes of manifestation, and clear white as the Radiant Core of all light frequencies.

Just to find someone who wrote openly about these inner lights was enormously validating to me. The Christian literature includes discussions of lights, but in a very cursory manner. Yet, for one experiencing kundalini, these lights cannot be ignored. Looking into them is, in itself, a kind of training for the attention, for when gazing into the lights, there is no thinking. In this way, then, the lights function to reinforce states of attention (samadhi) that transcend thinking.

The physiological basis of this inner seeing still escapes me, for it feels as though the eyes that see these inner lights are not the sensory eyes, but "inner eyes." These inner eyes continue to see through the sensory eyes after meditation. My only hypothesis is that following the piercing of the fifth chakra, the visual center of the brain or the pineal body sees the changing patterns of brain waves "in color."

Inner seeing is also reported by Gopi Krishna, who possessed the ability to view the current darting about in its ministerings to the various organs of the body. "It was intelligent, purposeful, an energy that knew what had to be achieved and was aware of all the conditions and rhythms and effects of my body. I knew every organ intimately and behaved in a manner that continued to sustain me through each day.... " I have not yet observed this, but I have no reason to doubt that Gopi Krishna observed the kundalini current moving throughout his body. How do we explain this? I'm not yet sure!

— Single-Seeing —

Following the transformation of the inner visual center and the nerves that feed it, one's ordinary mode of viewing things (with eyes open) changes dramatically. Everything seems sharp and clean, as though viewed against the background of a blue autumn sky. Occasionally, a bluish tinge or silvery luster outlines the object of perception. Simply walking about and looking around is an exquisite delight. There is no more need to create pleasurable circumstances, or worship experiences; one has only to "just-look," without thinking or analyzing, and the whole world is seen as a paradise.

If what is seen seems so different, it must also be said that the act of seeing, too, is different. As already mentioned, there is now a capacity to see things without thinking about them. This is a consequence of kundalini's effect on the relationship between the senses and the intellect (see chapter 3). Also, it feels as though the two sense eyes are seeing in union with a gigantic eye just internal to the forehead.

— Autonomic Functions —

Located on either side of the spinal cord is a "ladder" of nerves, which comprise the nerve trunks of the autonomic nervous system. While the central nervous system (brain, spinal cord, and their nerves) govern most voluntary activities, the autonomic nervous system is responsible for regulating the activities of glands, organs, and other involuntary processes. These two nervous systems communicate through nerve fibers along the spine.

As the kundalini current journeys up the spinal cord, it also flows outward into the autonomic nervous system. There, it stimulates the organs, glands, and other tissues, bringing healing and transformation unto its higher levels of frequency. In most cases, the increase of stimulation through sympathetic nerves is balanced by impulses from parasympathetic nerves, so that there is no net change in the level of activity of an organ — only in the amount of energy flowing through it. For example, the increase in stimulation to the pilomotor muscles (which "raise" the hairs) is balanced by inhibitory signals; if this were not the case, kundalini recipients could be identified on the basis of their hair standing straight up.

There are several notable exceptions to the above balancing activities, however, all pertaining to the sympathetic nerves.

1. The sympathetic nerves constrict blood vessels in the skin and most viscera. This leads to an increase in heart rate and faster breathing, both of which are observed during meditation. It may also explain the heat experienced on the skin — particularly on the shoulders. One is reminded here of yogis drying cold, wet sheets with their shoulders.

2. The sympathetic nerves dilate blood vessels in the skeletal muscles. This allows more blood to be taken to the skeletal muscles. Presumably, this once served as an adaptative role in running from danger. During kundalini, it serves to carry more nutrients to muscle tissues being healed from emotional pain.

3. Sympathetic nerves stimulate glycogenolysis, which increases blood sugar. This serves to keep the body energized in the state of heightened nervous activity. The Hindu's concern for proper diet may also be related to this effect.

4. Sympathetic nerves stimulate adrenalin secretion, which elevates heart rate and brings the body into a higher state of preparedness. This is also an undeniable effect of meditation, which, paradoxically, results in an eventual lowering of the threshold of excitability. Consequently, meditators do not become stressed easily.

There have been reports of the kundalini current coming up the spine in an unbalanced manner. Gopi Krishna believed that his initial awakening took place through the Pingala nadi, which corresponds to the right autonomic trunk. This almost drove him insane. It was not until he was able to direct the current up the sushumna nadi, the spinal canal, that he began to experience the positive effects of kundalini. The ideal in Kundalini Yoga is for the current to come up through the sushumna nadi, or spinal canal, from whence it enters the ventricles of the brain and eventually works its way to the top of the brain.

My thinking here is that it is indeed possible for the kundalini current to travel up the right or left trunk (or, in snake-like fashion, to dance back and forth). The result would be excessive stimulation of the autonomic nervous system, which would throw the entire organism into a severe upheaval! If the current would not subside spontaneously, then insanity would surely result.

What is most interesting to me is that the kundalini current can be directed by meditation. In Kundalini Yoga, one is taught to envision the current rising up through the cord in a form of liquid light. This exercise has been found helpful in directing the current up the center of the spine.

In my own case, I believe I suffered from an unbalanced kundalini current. Exercises such as the one described above helped me to "direct" the current up through the spinal cord, thus allowing the process to continue safely.

— Trance —

There is not much to say about this, except that following the piercing of the fifth chakra, the kundalini current entering the brain must in some manner stimulate the center of the brain that governs sleep. During prayer, one enters very quickly into a very deep state of meditation similar to sleep, yet one is awake all the while.

This deep, sleep-like trance produces tranquility and a sense of timelessness during the long periods of quiet that one must endure during the kundalini process. I have experienced this state throughout the process.

— Healing of Emotional Pain —

There should be no doubt in anyone's mind that emotional pain is stored in bodily tissues. Popular sayings such as "He gives me a pain in the neck!" or "She makes me sick to my stomach!" attest to this truth. Ulcers, high blood pressure, lower back pains, headaches, neck aches, and many other bodily ailments result from unexpressed, unresolved emotional pain. In soaking up these destructive energies, the body becomes weakened.

As the kundalini current circulates in the body, emotional energy that has been stored in bodily tissues through repression becomes "shaken loose." I picture this process as analogous to the role of fever in fighting a bacterial infection: the purpose of the fever is to create an environment that is inhospitable to the bacterium. Likewise, the kundalini current creates an environment that is incompatible with emotional pain. The tissues are forced to release their malevolent cargo, and then come the tears, sighing, and other forms of release. As a process for healing, kundalini offers tremendous potential.

— Asanas —

As electricity flows through a copper wire to a light bulb, it encounters in the light bulb filaments that partially resist its flow. These filaments begin to glow, emanating heat and light as the current passes through them.

I believe it is much the same with kundalini. The awakening of kundalini results in a more intense pattern of activity in the nervous system. As the kundalini current moves through the body, it encounters various kinds of resistance in bodily tissues: emotional pain, poisonous chemicals from foods, unhealed cuts, "germ" infections, bruises, etc. When the kundalini current encounters these hurting tissues, one can actually feel a kind of heat generated in these areas. Often, too, there is a rippling in the tissues as the current finally breaks through a pocket of resistance. These experiences are usually deliciously painful.

Sometimes, in order to facilitate the action of kundalini in overcoming a resistance, a group of muscles will contract slowly and deliberately. One may resist this process, but in sleep or deep meditation, the contracting muscles will have their way with or without one's permission. This is, I believe, part of the explanation for the spontaneous asanas frequently experienced during the kundalini process. Sannella also speculates that asanas result from the action of the kundalini current deep in the motor cortex and thalamic regions of the brain.

Whatever the cause, I can say that these asanas are often amazing. Most of those I experienced were focused on the facial and abdominal regions. There were a few nights, however, when I awoke to find an arm or leg twisting in a most peculiar fashion. One night, my right arm made an unbelievable circular motion behind my back and over my head. When I woke up, I noted in amazement the completion of this asana.

Dr. Sannella, Gopi Krishna, and others have hypothesized — rightly, I believe — that the origin of the various asanas practiced in Hatha Yoga derives from observation of the asanas produced during the early phases of a kundalini awakening. It was thought that by consciously and deliberately practicing these asanas, one could reduce the pockets of resistance to be encountered in the much-hoped-for event of a kundalini awakening. One could, as it were, lovingly prepare the body to receive its new and precious energies. Today, however, it seems that many practitioners of Hatha Yoga have lost this awareness of the relationship between kundalini and the asanas that they so diligently practice each day.

— Completing the Cycle —

Since 1975, when I emerged from a severe emotional Dark Night of the Soul, I have been addicted to morning prayer. If I missed my quiet time, I experienced tightness in my stomach and nausea. With the completion of the kundalini process, however, my abdominal area is constantly relaxed, even though I take very little time for deep meditation.

Dr. Lee Sannella theorizes that after the kundalini current completes its work in the brain, it travels down to the navel plexus area, where it finally terminates. This has been my experience.

I believe there must be a feedback mechanism of some kind between the brain and the navel plexus, directed by the medulla through the vagus nerve, which wanders around the body. When emotional stress begins to accumulate in the abdominal area, the muscles tighten. This information stimulates the pons area of the brain to produce a breathing pattern that intensifies the kundalini current. The nervous system is revved up, the emotional pain is cleared away (barring complications produced by the stubbornness of the conscious mind), and the navel plexus again communicates freely with the brain.

On a strictly physiological level, then, the purpose of all those thousands of hours of meditation during the past four years has been to establish this feedback loop between the brain and the navel plexus according to the frequency of kundalini energy. As this loop was being established, many pockets of resistance had to be overcome, and this was painful and confusing to me — mostly because of my ignorance of what was happening. But once they were overcome, the nervous system entered permanently into a state of higher functioning. All day long now, I experience my brain "meditating" automatically. My breathing patterns change as needed, and my volitional energies now move in harmony with this process. Glossalalia also plays a role in this process.

With the completion of the feedback loop, my feeling self also returned. Now I feel normal, myself, quite ordinary. Only there is a lightness of spirit I had experienced only occasionally in the past — the lightness of the golden-boy Christ-child.

— Conclusions —

Perhaps the most unique dimension of the kundalini experience is the physiological. Other psychological and spiritual growth processes are also accompanied by physiological changes, to be sure. But it is the physiological dimension that is most spectacular and undeniable in kundalini. Inner lights, chirping sounds, popping nerves, involuntary muscular movements, pressures and tingling sensations in the brain, fluttering sensations in the genital region, experiences of heat and cold in different parts of the body — these and other symptoms will be experienced at some time during the kundalini process.

This chapter has made use of Bentov's model to explain the anatomical and physiological basis of the kundalini current. I am aware that there are other explanations for the kundalini current — such as the uncoiling of the psycho-physiological energies repressed when the Ego began its flight from the body. These experiences of uncoiling cannot be denied. But one must ask from whence comes the "push" to uncoil these repressed energies. Bentov's model provides the answer to this, by proposing that intensifying currents in the sensory cortex increase the amount of electrical energy in those parts of the body stimulated by the cortex, where the energy is coiled. This cortical stimulation is increased in meditation, when the heartbeat slows and strengthens, causing the aorta to vibrate more intensely. One can experience this change in heartbeat during meditation, as well as the changes in cerebral activity that follow.

If Bentov's model is correct (and I am certainly not canonizing it here, but only saying that so far, it's the best explanation we have), then it follows that it ought to be possible to teach the physio-kundalini. This would involve focusing on meditation practices that strengthen the heartbeat. The abdominal breathing advocated in yoga and Zen provides precisely this spark. The asanas, or body postures taught in Hatha Yoga, also facilitate the uncoiling of repressed psycho-physiological energy in the joints and nerve plexus areas. Such practices focusing on breathing and asanas can be found in Kundalini Yoga. Therefore, the state of consciousness which results from the awakening of kundalini can be attained through one's own efforts. This single factor distinguishes kundalini from contemplative prayer, which cannot be attained on one's own. One can experience kundalini phenomena without contemplation; or one can experience contemplation with kundalini, such as I have done, or without kundalini phenomena, as many are doing.

At this time, I cannot recommend to anyone the pursuit of kundalini awakening outside a spiritual context, and without the supervision of a trained teacher. For awhile, I was convinced that kundalini itself would bring about moral and spiritual regeneration in a recipient, but I am no longer so sure of this. Several experts have called my attention to the fact that kundalini teachers can be found whose lifestyle is greatly at odds with Christian moral principles. Because these teachers espouse a moral system that allows for, say, promiscuous sexual activities, then such activities do not bring them to guilt. It is emotional pain (shame, guilt, fear, resentment) that makes kundalini very painful. But we must admit that what causes people emotional pain is relative to their values system.

At this stage in our reflection, then, we can see that the kundalini experience may or may not be a testament to the working of the Spirit. In Galatians 5:22–23, St. Paul lists the fruits of the Spirit as "love, joy, peace, patient endurance, kindness, generosity, faith, mildness, and chastity." In contrast, the fruits of kundalini are freedom from emotional pain, Ego-transcendence, psychic powers, expanded awareness, and heightened creativity. The fruits of kundalini may or may not be used in the service of the Spirit; indeed, they may be used for malevolent means.

It follows, then, that kundalini is an experience of our natural, human psycho-physiological powers. They are, we might say, soul powers, which lie dormant, or repressed, in those living out of a Mental Egoic consciousness. For those living in the Spirit-centered Ego, these energies are becoming more available, but it is not until the Ego is regressed that the kundalini energies become "uncoiled," or active.

Because the regression of the Ego is not necessarily accomplished in the service of Transcendence, it follows that the kundalini symptoms might also be observed in those experiencing psychoses and personality disorders. This needs to be studied.

Mike Milner has also alerted me to the possibility that Ego regressions do not always result in a new synthesis between the unconscious and conscious poles — that, in certain cases, it seems that the Ego has stretched itself to take in the unconscious. It is possible, in other words, that Ego-maniacs might have kundalini powers working in the service of Ego, rather than in the service of the Spirit. Gopi Krishna, Gene Kieffer, and others have attributed the works of such malevolent geniuses as Napoleon and Hitler to kundalini. This is another reason to avoid considering kundalini as a sure sign of the Holy Spirit.

It must be acknowledged that the ancient writers on kundalini were aware of these dangers, and I certainly do not wish to leave the impression that Kundalini Yoga is a malevolent science. Teachers of Kundalini Yoga such as Swami Radha and Swami Sivananda advocate moral character and faith in God along with the meditations and asanas that help to awaken kundalini. Gopi Krishna, Ramakrishna, Meher Baba, and Da Love Ananda — all great teachers drawing from the Hindu tradition — also advocate a strong love of God and neighbor. It seems that much of the secrecy surrounding kundalini in the East was undertaken to insure that those who awakened these energies had been properly disciplined in moral and spiritual principles so that this power would be used for good. Perhaps it was thought that by "broadcasting" the practices that awakened this energy — such as is happening today — this power might then become available to people of ill will. Whatever the case, the secret practices are well "out of the closet," and their effectiveness can be observed by any scientists interested in exploring virtually uncharted territory.

— *Chapter 4* —

SPIRITUALITY AND KUNDALINI

You're hit, old pipe, just
To clear ashes, not because
You're hated. See, you're
Kissed — because loved!

One could write tomes of reflection on the kundalini process and never say it better than this haiku. Indeed, this old pipe was hit, and the ashes cleared away were the emotional scars of thirty-five years of consciousness distortion. The stunning insight of the haiku, however, is the part about being kissed. It was the kiss of contemplative prayer that formed the context of my experiences of kundalini.

— Contemplative Prayer —

What possessed me to sit for long periods of time each day, grimacing through asanas, weeping copiously, gazing into inner lights, or sinking into depths of darkness and mystery impossible to describe? If I had known anything about kundalini, I could be accused of consciously intensifying the process to experience the bliss described by the yogis. As I have already written many times, however, I knew nothing about kundalini until the cycle was almost complete. For me, then, the awakening of kundalini took place in a very different context than yoga. My own interpretation is that kundalini arose in the context of contemplative prayer.

Before proceeding with reflections on the relationship between kundalini and contemplation, I think it necessary to clarify what I mean when I use the term "contemplative prayer." The word "contemplation" is used these days to describe a wide range of affective and silent prayer forms. While silence and affective energies are certainly part of my prayer, I prefer to reserve the term "contemplation" for those experiences of prayer that are passive rather than active. Contemplation, to me, was a sense of being grasped by God in the depths of my being in what I called the Still Point, the "place" where God and I intermingled in Spirit — the God/Self-Center. This union was sometimes confirmed through affective consolations, but even in the absence of consolation there remained a sense of union. Also, this resting in the Still Point was something I did in silence during my prayer times, but the resting and energizing went on all day, even during noisy periods. Therefore, silence and affective love for God do not approach the essence of contemplation in the sense that I use this word (which is the sense in which St. John of the Cross also uses the term). It is the sense of being grasped by God that is the essence of contemplation. One becomes aware that there is nothing to do to effect this union except to avoid sin and gently to turn the attention toward God; God does the rest, without need of any discursive meditation on our part.

One important feature of my own experience of contemplation has been the Pentecostal gift of tongues, or glossalalia. While resting in the Still Point, it frequently happened that the gentle, joyful, nonsensical babbling that is glossalalia arose spontaneously and served to deepen my sense of union with God. For those who do not know this experience, glossalalia seems a great mystery. I will say, however, that this spontaneity can be suppressed; although presenting itself spontaneously as an energy arising from the depths, one is not "possessed" by glossalalia. Learning to be open to this form of prayer has helped to deepen my experience of contemplation. During times of darkness, when kundalini was taking me down bewildering twists and turns and affective consolations were nowhere to be found, the presence of glossalalia gave me reassurance that the Holy Spirit was still directing the process.

And so I sat, day in and day out, resting in the Still Point, pray-ing in tongues occasionally, allowing the Spirit literally to drag me through the kundalini process. Deeper and deeper, the Still Point sank down into the unconscious, finally disappearing altogether. The final disappearance took place toward the end of the Adjust-ment phase, around December 1988, shortly before I discovered the literature on kundalini. It was to be several months before I discovered that the God/Self-Center was now everywhere, and that contemplation is just being-here-now-in-love.

— Contemplation and Physiology —

I am sure that everyone has suffered the experience of being brought down emotionally after communicating with someone who is depressed or in distress. This is a problem with which even the best of therapists must contend. I have no doubt that physiolog-ical consequences ensue from allowing ourselves to be emotionally disturbed by the problems of others.

The converse is also true. We have all, at times, experienced an emotional lift after conversing with a happy person, or af-ter listening to inspired music or preaching. One of the primary reasons people gather in churches on Sundays is in the hope of an emotional lift. Surely, too, there are positive physiological consequences that accompany our experiences of joy and peace.

What, then, might we expect to happen to the physiology of a person who, day after day for years, spends an hour or so each morning resting in the experience of union with God? Supposing that God, or Christ, *is* a real Being with real Energies that can affect a human being. Then does it not follow that the physiology of a human being will be affected as a consequence of union with God?

In the language of the haiku with which we began this chapter, we can say that contemplation is being kissed by God. To appre-ciate the relationship between kundalini and contemplation, we have only to reflect upon what happens when two lovers kiss one another. There are many psychological and physiological conse-quences, none the least of which is sexual arousal. In expressing their love through kisses and embraces, these lovers may even-tually have intercourse. In the act of intercourse, we see spiritual, psychological, and physiological processes working together to ef-fect a profound sense of union between two lovers in the flesh.

This is analogous to what happens in contemplation; for the contemplative, kundalini is the psycho-physiological consequence of a spiritual union with God. In a spiritual context, the purpose of kundalini can be viewed in terms of opening the person to a deeper experience of union with God.

Just as it is possible for two lovers to indulge in intercourse primarily for the physical sensations and outside of a context of love, so, too, is it possible to activate the kundalini process through breathing and asanas outside of a context of contemplation. As with fornication, the consequence of this indulgence is a kind of self-centeredness — only of a much more deadly and insidious kind than one finds among fornicators. After I learned about kundalini, I sometimes became more focused on intensifying my experiences of kundalini energy than I did on praising God. This was an awful sin — a kind of spiritual masturbation that was, rightly, punished through the consequences of spiritual stagnation, and a very big headache.

Although kundalini as a physiological process can be explained rather well using Bentov's hypotheses, this should in no way lead us to conclude that kundalini is merely a physiological phenomenon. The euphoria of sexual intercourse can be explained in terms of glands and chemicals and stimulating the pleasure centers of the brain, but this tells us nothing about the psychological and spiritual dimensions of sex. As most partners have discovered, sex that is experienced only for physical pleasure turns out, in the long run, to be not so pleasurable at all. So, too, kundalini that is experienced outside of a spiritual context is generally short-lived and most unenjoyable. It was for this reason, no doubt, that the ancient texts on Kundalini Yoga describe the process of transformation in terms of the stirring of the goddess Shakti and her movement toward union with the Lord Shiva. Divorced from a religious context of this kind, kundalini can become a very destructive force.

— The Nature of the Dynamic Ground —

Throughout this text, I have used the term "Dynamic Ground," following Michael Washburn (1989). I have spoken of the Ground as the energy of the Soul and have stated that with respect to its relationship with God, it is not-one (not-God), but not-two (not separate from God). To me, these are not merely speculations, but facts of experience, as I will now explain.

One of the first things I noted in my journal about kundalini energy — before I even knew the name for the experience — was that it was simultaneously "of me, but not-me." I could assume an attitude toward it; it was a trans-Egoic force. And yet, at the same time, it was very much "of me"; it was both psychic energy and libido, sexual energy, which belong to my experience. Hence, I concluded that this energy arose from a depth where the physiological and psychological came together.

But this was not all, for I also experienced a spiritual dimension to kundalini. After all, this experience was triggered and intensified as a consequence of prayer, and so it seemed to move in response to the loving graces of God. Kundalini was "of-God," and yet, because it was also "of-me," there was no doubt that kundalini was not-God.

This, then, is how kundalini feels: "of-me, but not-me"; and "of-God, but not-God." I could think of only one Source capable of generating such an energy, and that is the Soul.

In Catholic theology, it is held that the Soul is the life principle of the body; there is no living body without the Soul. But neither is there a human experience of the Soul apart from the body. Body and Soul are one; a person is an embodied Soul.

The Soul is a creation of God; it is not-God. But neither is the Soul separate from God; it stands in relation to God as light to the sun. It is joined with God through the grace of God's creative will, apart from which it would not exist. Therefore, the Soul is a creation endowed with its own unique qualities and energies; it is a human Soul. It is capable of realizing its dependence upon and union with God, and, in so doing, realizing its true nature. But, on the level of consciousness — especially Egoic consciousness — it is capable of losing awareness of its union with God, and so living in fear and delusion.

My experiences of kundalini confirm, for me, this brief overview of Catholic metaphysics. I would say that kundalini is an energy from the Ground, which is the "place" where the energies of the body and Soul are one. Kundalini is, then, a kind of primal human energy, simultaneously impacting the physiological, psychological, and spiritual levels of human existence. It is a Soul energy, for it is the Soul that gives life to the body in all its dimensions. The awakening of kundalini signals the awakening of the powers of the Soul in the body. Whether this is for good or evil is another question altogether.

— Sinful Realities —

The view of the Soul and its relation to body and God that I have shared above is not held in the East. In Hinduism, for example, it is held that Brahman (the transcendent God) equals Atman (the immanent God). Catholics would agree that God's presence can be experienced within the Soul, but would staunchly deny that the Soul is God. This distinction is important, for it helps to clarify the significance of kundalini in the spiritual life. It is one thing to say that kundalini is an energy of the Ground, or body-Soul union, and quite another to say that it is the Holy Spirit. Because Hindus do not recognize the existence of a Soul that is both one with God and a creation of God (not-God), they naturally conclude, as Swami Muktananda and Gopi Krishna have done, that kundalini is really the same thing as the Christian experience of the Holy Spirit.

What we think about the nature of God's relation to the Soul also affects our understanding of sin. It is the view of Hindu yogis that there is no sin for enlightened individuals. A Catholic woman I know who has experienced kundalini and claims now to have no-self (even no Soul!) also says the same for herself: that she is incapable of sin. Given the Catholic understanding of Soul, and the contention advanced herein that kundalini is an energy of the Ground, we see that awakening of kundalini does not in any way signal the end of sin. A harmonious integration of kundalini will lead to higher states of consciousness, psychic gifts, creativity, and inner freedom. The cleansing of emotional pain will also diminish the split between the Ego and the Ground. Having experienced all these fruits, I can still say, however, that one is not free from sin — understood from a Christian viewpoint, that is.

The experience of Da Love Ananda comes to mind here. He worked hard for years at the various yogas, studying under great Hindu masters, including Swami Muktananda. The fruit of all this was a highly awakened kundalini, great psychic gifts, and pure, nonreflective awareness (nirvikalpa samadhi). Yet he realized that something was missing. For one thing, his human relationships were not very close; it seemed that his enlightenment served only to distance him from others. After struggling with this tension for years, he came to the realization that God is Love, and that love of God and others is the great blessing.

What I conclude from my reading and experience is that the higher states of consciousness are no indications of holiness. Just as it is possible for the Mental Ego to serve God or mammon, so it is with the trans-Egoic states. For God is Love, and Love is not simply a state of consciousness. Rather, love is an *orientation* of consciousness that wishes happiness for all and is willing to become involved in the struggles of others. Some of the acclaimed spiritual masters of our times give evidence to the blessings of love; others demonstrate what appears to be an insidious kind of selfishness. The higher states of consciousness bring greater freedom, but this freedom does not compulsively move one to charity. Love is a life stance — a decision that one must reaffirm until death settles the matter forever.

— Spiritual Disciplines —

When I discovered the Hindu literature on kundalini, I was struck by the similarities between the disciplines in Kundalini Yoga and those that I put forth in my book *Pathways to Serenity*. I wrote *Pathways* in 1987, during the early phases of the awakening of kundalini. It seemed at that time immensely important for me to find a way to live that helped me to focus all the activities of my consciousness — sensing, thinking, feeling, intuiting, perceiving, desiring, remembering — in accord with the love of God, self, and neighbor. The Twelve Steps of Alcoholics Anonymous, the Four Noble Truths of Buddhism, and the Spiritual Exercises of St. Ignatius of Loyola had helped me tremendously through the years. *Pathways* represents a synthesis of the principles articulated in these different approaches to spiritual growth.

The Hindu literature on kundalini helped me to appreciate how important was this foundation of discipline. Kundalini is like a highly-charged elixir that is poured into a very delicate and fragile vessel. If there are leaks or weak spots in the vessel, then the elixir will be lost and the vessel itself will be hurt by the powerful energy being discharged. Given a healthy vessel, however, kundalini can be harnessed to do a mighty work on earth. Therefore, one must learn to take proper care of the earthen vessel in which we pass our days. One must also take special care to discipline the senses, which are the places where energy enters into and flows out of the vessel.

All these concerns had been strongly impressed on me during the early stirrings of kundalini. When I read through the disciplines described in Swami Radha's classical work, *Kundalini Yoga for the West,* I experienced a thorough validation of the disciplines in *Pathways to Serenity.* I appreciated the emphasis on awareness as a key to growing in discipline. "Be-here-now-in-love," and "do what you're doing" had been my guiding phrases; Kundalini Yoga emphasized these attitudes and more.

Given the similarities in disciplines, I must nonetheless acknowledge that I am operating out of a very different theological perspective than that which informs Kundalini Yoga. We shall explore these differences more fully in chapter 5.

— Stages of Spiritual Growth —

The primary concern of spirituality is in directing the will of a human being toward its true end, which is knowing, loving, and serving God. Although the will may be focused in many directions, experience demonstrates that there is, in every person, one predominating Center of meaning and value that takes priority over other centers. This Center is called "the heart" in Scripture. It is from the heart, or volitional Center of consciousness, that one's thoughts, feelings, and desires spring. "Where your treasure is, there is your heart," said Jesus (Matt. 6:21). What we place in the Center makes all the difference, for one's life ultimately takes its shape around this Center.

The spirituality presented in Kundalini Yoga describes seven centers of consciousness in association with the seven chakras as follows:

> *First Chakra.* Security.
>
> *Second Chakra.* Pleasure.
>
> *Third Chakra.* Power and Ambition.
>
> *Fourth Chakra.* Personal Responsibility.
>
> *Fifth Chakra.* Conceptual Discrimination.

Sixth Chakra. Conscious Awareness.

Seventh Chakra. Fully-awakened Soul.

In developing its spirituality along these lines, disciplines are presented that aim to help one move from the lower to the higher centers of consciousness. The ancient Hindu texts also encourage meditation on certain symbols and sounds associated with each chakra.

Because my own spiritual journey has followed a trajectory almost identical to that presented above, I am inclined to agree with the stages of growth described in Kundalini Yoga. A problem for me, however, is that I sincerely doubt that these centers of consciousness are actually situated in the chakras, as most New Age writers insist. Rather, it seems that this is merely a way of structuring a spirituality along organic lines. Swami Radha's book, *Kundalini Yoga for the West,* seems to take this approach, and Yogi Bhajan says as much in *Kundalini: Meditation Manual for Intermediate Students:*

> Yes, Kundalini is known as the nerve of the soul. This is to be awakened. Your soul is to be awakened. When soul gets awakened, there remains nothing. What else?
> In the practical reality, these chakras are imaginary and nothing else. The Kundalini is just a Kundalini and nothing else. It is not very important.... We use these terms simply to make the process clear so we can get on with it.

Of course, on the level of physiology, the chakras (as spinal plexus centers) are very real. When used in the context of spirituality, however, "these chakras are imaginary and nothing else." They are "places" in consciousness.

The purpose of spiritual disciplines, then, is to help one move from the lower centers to the higher centers of consciousness. In making this journey, one becomes increasingly free. Operating out of the fourth center, for example, one is able to direct the desires for pleasure, power, and security in a self-chosen and responsible manner. In moving to the fifth center, responsibility is brought into greater clarity through wisdom. The True Self begins to awaken in the sixth center, and the awakened Soul is experienced in the seventh center.

Traditionally, Catholic mystical writers have spoken of three stages of spiritual growth:

1. *Purgative*. A time of struggle in which false centers are rejected, but they are also still attractive. One experiences an intense civil war, but begins progressing in virtue.

2. *Illuminative*. One finds it less difficult to resist temptation. One's true center is God, and one works at progressing in virtue and understanding.

3. *Unitive*. The person is united with God in his/her Center. Virtue comes easily, although the possibility of sin remains.

Initially, it seems to me that the chakra system and the three stages above were saying the same thing. Now, I am not so sure. There are parallels, to be sure. But it seems that the chakra system is more concerned with states of consciousness while the three stages above are concerned with the degree of the experience of union with God. As we discussed earlier, states of consciousness do not guarantee a deeper union with God.

Having said this, we must acknowledge that there is also great overlap between the seven chakra consciousnesses and the three Christian stages. In reading the lives of Christian mystics, one will generally find that their growth in union with God was accompanied by growth into the higher states of consciousness. As they progressed in union, they ascended the chakras as well, manifesting greater psychic gifts, creativity, and inner freedom. This expanded consciousness served to deepen their experience of unity and to enhance the effectiveness of their ministry. With the saints, however, there was always the awareness that psychic gifts were one thing and holiness, or union with God, another.

Catholic mystics have also described Dark Nights of the Soul in the spiritual journey. These are times of turmoil, when the psychophysiological energies are changing to open the Soul to a fuller experience of union with God. I have experienced two of these Dark Nights in my life: the first in 1974–75, and the second which I am describing in this book.

The first Dark Night was deeply emotional and brought me from the fourth to the fifth center of consciousness, where I operated for years out of a Spirit-centered Ego state. I published eleven books (and wrote many others), offered retreats and workshops, counseled people in trouble, and was quick to engage myself in any discussion that might result in advancing the faith. There was lots of spiritual energy in this state. Even so, such a consciousness was still unbalanced; I was very much "in my head," and my degree of union was limited by Ego.

The consciousness resulting from the Night of Kundalini moves between the sixth and seventh centers. In comparison to the state I experienced between 1975 and 1986, it is more balanced and holistic. I continue to experience the energies of the lower centers, but now they fall into line in accordance with the energies of the sixth and seventh centers. In the context of this discussion of centers of consciousness, I can see that one of the works of kundalini has been to "raise the center" of consciousness to allow for a fuller experience of union with God.

— Convergence and Divergence among Mystics —

An issue that has haunted me for a long time has to do with the experiences of mystics from the various world religions. One of my all-time favorite books is *The Perennial Philosophy*, by Aldous Huxley. The position taken by Huxley is that the mystics of the world's religions are all seeing the .ame vision and that the world's religions are different paths to this vision. He divides the book into various themes and compares quotes on these themes by mystics from the world religions to demonstrate that they are all really saying the same thing. Although I love this book and have read it many times, I nonetheless have lingering questions about the convergence of religious experiences. Although the similarities cannot be denied, it seems to me that Huxley has glossed over the differences, which are considerable.

My experiences with kundalini during the past three years have not resolved my questions about convergence and divergence among the world's religions, but they have brought greater clarity concerning some of the issues at stake. Some of these issues, which I have already discussed, concern the relationships between the higher state of consciousness and union with God, contemplation and enlightenment, sin and virtue. But a final issue, and the most mysterious of all, concerns the Soul itself.

Earlier in this chapter, we reflected briefly on the difference between the Catholic view of the Soul and the Hindu view of Atman. The chief distinction, we noted, was that the Soul, while one-with-God, is nevertheless not-God. The significance of this insight relative to kundalini is that the Soul awakening which kundalini signals may or may not bring about a deeper union with God, for union with God is effected through love and surrender and not through conscious awareness. The Soul is a creation that may realize itself at the level of the Dynamic Ground, where it is one with the body and with God. This is, I believe, the enlightenment experience, a natural (perhaps original) state of human consciousness available to all who will undertake the right kinds of disciplines.

What I wonder most about is how people experience God at the level of the Ground. God being one and the same for all, do all experience God in the same way, as Huxley suggests? Does the quality of faith we possess make a difference in our experience of God at the level of Ground? To what extent does one's theological outlook affect the experience of God? And how about the kind of life one has led all along? Is the Ground a pure experience of Reality waiting, in undefiled manner, to reveal itself in a non-Egoic consciousness? Or does the spiritual work undertaken by Ego in some manner "till the soils" of the Ground? Surely the Ego distorts our experience of the Ground! But does the Ego affect the Ground itself?

These are all questions which remain, and to which, I am aware, there may be no definitive answers. My suspicion is that the Ego does affect the Ground — so much so that the Soul energy can be permanently distorted through sinful living. This, at least, is implied in the Catholic doctrine on Hell. If we recall that the Ego is the conscious representative of the Ground, then it follows that the Ego can affect the Ground. It also follows that the faith-attitudes of the Ego can help to open the Ground to the transcendental energies of God. This, at least, is what the paradigm we have been using suggests, and my experiences confirm this.

— The Cosmic Christ —

My Christian experiences with kundalini have brought me to the realization that Christ is the one "through whom all things came into being, and apart from whom nothing came to be" (John 1:3). Prior to the regression of the Ego that brought to surface the kundalini energies, I experienced Christ as the center of my Ego. The

Holy Spirit was experienced as a healing and loving energy arising from the Ground (and beyond) to animate the Christ center
and move the Ego to experiences of ecstatic praise. This union between the Christo-centric Ego and the Holy Spirit was felt to be
the "place" where consciousness rested against unconsciousness.
In the Spirit-centered Ego, I experienced a deep unity with creation. I knew that Creation was "of-God, but not-God," but my
experience of God-in-creation was felt largely on an unconscious
level. At the level of consciousness, rivers were still rivers, trees
were trees, and mountains were mountains.

With the regression and rebirth that has taken place, the Spirit-
centered Ego has evolved to the True Self experience described in
chapter 2. There is no internal center in this True Self; rather, the
Ground itself flows throughout the whole person, sees through the
person — is the whole person. As a Christian, I experience the life
of the Ground as Christ. My Soul lives by His Spirit; He animates
the energies of the Ground itself, largely through the Sacrament
of the Eucharist. There are times when I have a definite conviction
that the one who peers out of my eyes is not me, but Christ, or,
I should say, Phil-Christ. This "seeing-in Christ" has brought a
dramatic change in my experience of creation. No longer is there
an unconscious sense of God's presence in creation; now it seems
that creation itself is God-manifest. Trees are still trees, rivers are
rivers, and mountains are mountains. But they are also Christ.

I am convinced that kundalini has facilitated this mystical,
cosmic consciousness by "rewiring" my senses. No longer do
sense perceptions feed through the intellect; no longer are there
"thoughts in my eyeballs," interfering with my perceptions, as of
old. Now there is just-seeing, just-smelling, just-tasting — and all
this intelligently, with a silent mind.

How sweet it is — this enlightenment experience! How joyful! How freeing! No longer is there any sense of alienation, for
the Ground that flows throughout my being is identical with the
Reality of all creation. It seems that the mystics of all the world's
religions know something of this. Knowing the Christ dimension
of this experience brings me additional joy, however. Would that
all could know this life to the full!

— *Chapter 5* —

CHRISTIANITY AND KUNDALINI

Every religion includes accounts of the awakening of kundalini. Among the Hopi Indians, for example, F. Waters, in his *Book of the Hopi*, writes of their belief in vibratory centers located along the spine, which echoed the sounds of the universe. "The first of these in man lay at the top of the head. Here, when he was born, was the soft spot, ko'pavi, the 'open door' through which he received his life and communicated with his Creator." Other centers are listed in the center of the forehead, the throat, the heart, and, finally, the navel. "The last of man's important centers lay under his navel, it was the throne in man of the Creator himself. From it he directed all the functions of man." As we discussed in chapter 2, the kundalini cycle is regulated from the solar plexus.

During the course of my research on this work, I came across accounts of energy centers and disciplines for awakening kundalini (not always so named, of course) in Buddhism and Taoism as well. The Taoist chakras are almost identical to those described in Hinduism. Taoism also makes use of sexual practices to raise the energy of consciousness in a manner similar to Tantric Hindu practices. Buddhism, on the other hand, emphasizes celibacy as the way to transform sexual energy to pure consciousness. The various states of enlightenment described in Tantric, Buddhist, and

Taoist literature seem very similar, attesting again to a common experience.

What about experiences of kundalini in the other great branch of the world's religions — the Judeo-Christian-Islam branch? To be sure, these religions take a very different approach to salvation. Where Eastern religions begin with the human being reaching out to the divine, Western religions begin with the divine reaching out to humans. Eastern religions emphasize practices that transform the human to a divine being; Western religions emphasize divine grace as the transforming energy, without which human beings remain little more than beasts. The East offers sophisticated spiritual "technologies," specifically designed to divinize the person; the West offers very little in the way of "how-to" spirituality, emphasizing instead faith and love. The East regards the Ego as an obstacle to the experience of God; the West sees grace working in and through the Ego to bring about transformation. The East holds that absolute nonduality is the highest level of consciousness; the West seldom drifts far from duality in its descriptions of relationship with the divine. Given these and many other differences between Eastern and Western religions, it is obvious that the metaphysics and spiritualities of these two great traditions should also differ.

— Kundalini in Christian Mysticism —

There is nothing in Christian teaching comparable to the Hindu notions of chakras, astral body, and kundalini energy. Neither will one find in Christianity anything like the spiritualities associated with the yoga system, which are designed to lead one up through the various centers to the experience of union. Nevertheless, the chakras, the astral body, and the awakening of kundalini are *experiences* that can be identified in the experiences of many, many Christian mystics. In contrast to the East, however, these experiences were not sought as means to union; they were experienced as a consequence of prayer.

Before going on to review the evidence of kundalini among the Christian mystics, I must mention a manuscript discovered by Gopi Krishna in 1978. Written by an Abbé N. de Montfauçon de Villars in Paris about three hundred years ago, this work, entitled *Comte de Gabalis*, has much to say about kundalini and Christianity and is often used as a reference by New Age folk to demonstrate that Jesus knew about Hinduism. As I was unable to locate this work, I quote it from Gene Kieffer's book *Kundalini for the New Age*, pages 8 and 9.

In the early Christian Church the word Christ was used as a synonym for the first solar principle in man. "But as Christ is in you, though your body must die because of sin, yet your spirit has life because of righteousness." Rm. 8, 10 . . . ["Solar principle" is a term frequently used in the book to signify kundalini.]

Allegory of Eve and the Serpent: The primordial electricity or solar force, semilatent with the aura of every human being, was known to the Greeks as the Speirema, the serpent coil; and in the Upanishads, the sacred writings of India, it is said to lie coiled up like a slumbering serpent. In the third chapter of the Book of Genesis it is symbolized as the serpent, "more subtle than any beast of the field that the Lord God had made." Eve, when this force stirred within her, was tempted to its misapplication. Directed downward through the lower physical centers for generation, unhallowed by a consciousness of responsibility to God and the incoming soul, the serpent force or Fire brought knowledge of evil; directed upward toward the brain for regeneration, the formation of the deathless solar body, it brought knowledge of good. Hence the dual operation of the solar force is symbolized as the tree of the knowledge of good and evil.

Kieffer and other writers, using quotes such as the one above, goes on in convergenist fashion to suggest that kundalini is really the primordial mystical experience common to all religions.

As anyone can see from the above quote, however, Abbé de Villars was familiar with sacred writings of India, which include many references to kundalini. Since his book also includes references to the philosopher's stone and the writings of alchemists, I conclude that the Abbé's work, far from representing a serious study of the spirituality of the early Church, was an attempt to synthesize common elements in occult writings. One finds nothing about Christ as the solar principle in early Christian writings.

A much more likely reference to the experience of kundalini

energy among Christian mystics can be found in *The Theology of Christian Perfection*, by Antonio Royo, O.P., and Jordan Aumann, O.P. Once a standard reference for Catholic religious, this book includes a chapter on extraordinary phenomena. These are considered strictly gratuitous phenomena or *gratiae gratis datae* (special charisms not necessary for salvation). "Nor, do we repeat, do all such manifestations proceed from a supernatural cause; many of them could be due to a mental, physical or nervous disorder; or they could be caused by diabolical power. On the other hand, when any of the following phenomena have God as their cause, they are usually found to occur in persons of a holy life." The authors then go on to list a wide variety of extraordinary mystical phenomena observed among saints. I am including here only those that have been associated with kundalini.

1. *Flames of Love*. Royo and Aumann speak here of the experiences of burning sensations in the body, considered to be signs of the mystic's love of God. They describe three levels: (a) simple interior heat, usually in the area of the heart; (b) intense ardors, intense heat that causes great discomfort; (c) material burning, which scorches the clothing and burns those whom the mystic touches. Sts. Philip Neri and Paul of the Cross experienced this.

2. *Tears of Blood and Bloody Sweat*. During times of intense kundalini heat, when emotions are being eliminated through tears, it is possible that blood vessels near the surface of the skin and in the tear ducts would rupture, reddening the sweat and tears. St. Lutgard, Blessed Christina, and several others are listed as recipients of this "gift." Christ at Gethsemane also experienced bloody sweat.

3. *Prolonged Absence of Sleep*. Because the kundalini current maintains the body in a state of freedom from emotional pain, one does not need sleep as in times past. Prayer accomplishes what sleep once did. St. Macarius, St. Lydwina, St. Peter Alcantara, St. Rose of Lima, and St. Catherine de Ricci are noted for going long periods without sleep.

4. *Bilocation*. This may or may not be related to kundalini, depending on whether we are speaking of the physical body or the astral body. Kundalini does not explain bilocation of

the physical body, but it can account for the energy that empowers the astral body to leave the physical body and roam about, where it might be seen by those with inner vision. St. Clement, St. Francis of Assisi, St. Anthony of Padua, St. Francis Xavier, St. Anthony Claret, and St. Alphonsus Liguori were noted for bilocating.

5. *Mystical Aureoles.* Experiences of inner light are commonly associated with kundalini, although it is rare that others should also see these aureoles. There are countless cases of aureoles: Moses, St. Ignatius Loyola, St. Philip Neri, St. Francis de Sales, St. Charles Borromeo, and St. John Vianney are famous examples. The artistic depictions of aureoles around saints in sacred paintings are an expression of this phenomenon.

6. *Incombustible Bodies.* This may be unrelated to kundalini. Nevertheless, there is no denying that kundalini transforms bodily tissues; one is seldom sick after undergoing the process. St. Peter Igneus, St. Dominic, and St. Catherine of Siena are examples.

7. *Bodily Elongation.* I suspect the work of kundalini in producing a body-stretching asana to be at issue here. Blessed Stephana Quinzani and St. Catherine of Genoa are examples.

In addition to the above, I recognize the work of kundalini in the spontaneous asanas (standing on head, bodily contortions, etc.) experienced by St. Thérèse of Lisieux, and in the temporary paralyses of limbs experienced by St. Teresa of Avila.

It is also possible that kundalini is related to stigmata. I frequently experience the kundalini current as a throbbing on the soles of my feet and the palm of my hand. Could the combination of kundalini and meditation on the wounds of Christ produce stigmata?

Numerous mystical phenomena of a psychic nature might also be related to kundalini. I do not believe that all psychics experience kundalini, and it is clear from my own case that kundalini does not always lead to profound psychic experience. Given a person with latent psychic gifts, however, it is certain that kundalini would enhance the experience of these gifts. This could help to explain experiences such as visions (clairvoyance), moving things without touching them (psychokinesis), hearing voices/revelations (clair-audience), healing, foretelling the future, reading another's heart, seeing auras, and other gifts. It is clear that many saints who experienced these psychic gifts also experienced kundalini.

— Dark Nights of the Soul —

During the journey of growth, many Christian mystics undergo periods of aridity and confusion described by St. John of the Cross as Dark Nights of the Soul. These are times when the psyche undergoes a profound change in its energy dynamics as a consequence of its deepening union with God through contemplative prayer. St. John describes two of these nights: of the senses, which most serious Christians experience, and of the spirit, which few are called to endure.

Because St. John wrote about the process of transformation in psychological and spiritual terms, it is difficult to ascertain whether kundalini played a role in what he describes. In reading St. John during my most intense times of kundalini upheaval, I often felt like I was reading my journal. One passage in particular stayed with me:

> For this night is gradually drawing the spirit away from its ordinary and common experience of things and bringing it nearer the Divine sense, which is a stranger and an alien to all human ways. It seems now to the soul that it is going forth from its very self, with much affliction. At other times it wonders if it is under a charm or a spell, and it goes about marvelling at the things that it sees and hears, which seem to it very strange and rare, though they are the same that it was accustomed to experience aforetime. (*Dark Night of the Soul*, Peers translation, p. 123)

I laughed out loud when I read this — something that a reader of St. John seldom feels moved to do! It is a perfect description of the psychological state that accompanies intense kundalini activity.

Interestingly, the best advice I ever read for coping with kundalini was also written by St. John. He urges those experiencing the Dark Night to an alert passivity to the working of the Holy Spirit. This calls for renouncing the effort to experience God through the use of discursive meditation (reflection, spiritual reading, conceptualizing, use of reason), since God wishes to communicate with the Soul directly. I now find such discursive meditation to be an immense obstacle to experiencing God — a throwback to an earlier time in my life. With such meditation comes extreme discomfort in my brain, as though the kundalini current is blocked by the activities of the intellect. Only total passivity to the kundalini current brings serenity. Only then, too, is there a sense of God's presence.

Because of the similarities between the psycho-spiritual states described by St. John of the Cross and those that I experienced during the kundalini process, I am inclined to say that kundalini is probably a factor at work during the various Dark Nights of the Soul described by St. John and other Christian mystics. This is not such a far-fetched proposition when we consider that any significant changes in one's psychological experience must of necessity be accompanied by changes in the physiology that supports it. It is this change in physiology that kundalini makes possible. I do not know why St. John and other Christian mystics did not write more about the physiological dimensions of their experiences. Perhaps their attention was focused elsewhere — on God, where it rightly belongs.

— Siddha Yoga and Pentecostalism —

A strong convergence between Hindu and Christian spirituality can be noted when comparing Siddha Yoga with Pentecostalism. In recent times, Swami Muktananda Paramahamsa was most prominent in spreading the practice of Siddha meditation. While reading through *Kundalini: The Secret of Life*, by Swami Muktananda, I was struck by the similarities it shares with Pentecostalism.

In Siddha Yoga, kundalini is awakened through the grace of the Master, or Guru. "The Guru and the spiritual energy which he awakens are identical," wrote Swami Muktananda. "Not only is it the Guru's task to awaken the Kundalini; he must also control and regulate the process until the disciple attains the ultimate realization of the Self, and help the disciple remove all the blocks which hinder his full spiritual development." And how does the Guru awaken kundalini? Through a graced touch from the Guru called Shaktipat, "when the Guru directly transmits his own divine Shakti (kundalini energy) into the disciple. It is the divine function of the

Guru to awaken the dormant Shakti; when the Guru transmits his power into a disciple, the inner aspect of Kundalini is automatically activated and set into operation."

There are many amazing stories about Swami Muktananda. He made frequent trips to America and attracted a large number of disciples, many of whom evidenced astonishing growth as a result of receiving Shaktipat from this Guru. One of my favorites is recounted in Dr. Lee Sannella's book, *The Kundalini Experience*, about a male psychiatrist who visited Swami Muktananda at his ashram in India. While meditating at the ashram, the psychiatrist experienced kundalini energy intensifying between his eyebrows, at the site of the sixth chakra. Sannella writes that "Swami Muktananda spontaneously walked over to him and immediately began to work his fingers over the space between the sixth center and the center at the crown of the head. Streams of kundalini energy started to flow in a V-shaped pattern toward the crown center. Since that time, he reports, the kundalini energy has rarely left the crown center." Not only did this Guru awaken kundalini, but he also helped to direct it toward a completion of its cycle.

Swami Muktananda states that there are four ways in which the Guru (or a representative authorized by the Guru) can transmit Shaktipat: by touch, word, look, and thought. The most common way is by touching the disciple, usually in the space between the eyebrows, but also in the area of the heart or at the base of the spine. Not everyone receives the same degree of awakening as a result of Shaktipat. A wide range of responses, from intense to mild to gentle can be observed.

In contrast to Hatha and Kundalini Yoga, where one undertakes specialized disciplines to awaken kundalini, Shaktipat brings about a quick and thorough transformation. As a result of Shaktipat, it frequently happens that one spontaneously practices the disciplines prescribed in other forms of yoga. "For instance," Swami Muktananda writes, "one may experience involuntary movements of the body, such as shaking and movements of the arms and legs. The head may even begin to rotate violently. One may automatically perform various yogic asanas, mudras, bandhas, and different kinds of pranayama, which are all parts of Hatha Yoga.... But when these movements occur spontaneously, you automatically perform only those postures which are necessary and appropriate" (for purification and transformation).

CHRISTIANITY AND KUNDALINI

All the other forms of yoga are also fulfilled during a kundalini transformation resulting from Shaktipat. The love and devotion emphasized by Bhakti Yoga occur spontaneously, as do deep insights (Jnana Yoga), detachment (Karma Yoga), and enlightenment (Raja Yoga). It should be noted, however, that in Siddha Yoga these activities are the *result* of the action of kundalini, and not its cause. In Siddha Yoga, the activity of kundalini is attributed to the grace of the Guru. Therefore, one does not have to practice complicated disciplines to maintain kundalini; the disciplines suggest (even impose!) themselves when appropriate. When kundalini is awakened through Hatha/Kundalini Yoga, it must be maintained through these practices. In contrast, Swami Muktananda writes, "Siddha Yoga is very easy, very natural. There are many paths through which you attain the final goal with great effort and difficulty, but in Siddha Yoga you attain it very naturally and spontaneously."

The fruit of the spirit observed as a result of Siddha Yoga is greater awareness, bliss, intuitive knowledge, and compassion. Many of Swami Muktananda'a followers live active lives in the world; Shaktipat does not lead to an inert kind of enlightenment. Because the grace of the Guru continues to work in the disciple even when they are apart, the transformation of the person by kundalini proceeds during the course of everyday living.

Those who are familiar with Pentecostal Christianity must surely be amazed by what I have just described. In Pentecostalism, too, we see evidence of the transmission of the spiritual energy through a special touch, usually the laying on of hands by the community, or by a bishop or minister. As a result of this "Christian Shaktipat," people frequently evidence spiritual gifts or charisms such as speaking in tongues (a Christian mantra?), prophesying, and healing. Great love for other people begins to well up in the heart. One also becomes deeply fond of spending time in prayer. These and other gifts come spontaneously and effortlessly as the Spirit prompts.

When people receive the laying on of hands at a Pentecostal or charismatic prayer service, it frequently happens that something like spontaneous asanas take place. In the South, Pentecostals have sometimes been called "holy rollers," a somewhat disrespectful reference to instances when people receiving the laying on of hands fall on the floor and shake or roll. During the years when I was involved in Catholic charismatic renewal, I saw this happen on many occasions. We called this "slaying in the Spirit," or "resting in the Spirit." Although I have never experienced this in dramatic fashion, I know for a fact that many people who have experienced this are basically healthy people. They described to me a sense of feeling overwhelmed by God's power and love, and feeling moved to lie still in a semitrance state as an incredibly blissful energy raced about in their bodies. Many reported healings in memory and body as a result of resting in the Spirit.

During the course of a Catholic charismatic prayer meeting I attended recently, I was asked to lay hands on people to pray with them for release from fear. To my utter amazement, person after person fell to the floor as I prayed with them. Most remained there for only a few seconds, but some stayed in a semitrance state for several minutes. One woman twitched and shook all over her body for about twenty minutes, babbling incessantly in glossalalia as she did. When she finally sat up, her face radiated a quality of peace and joy seldom observed among human beings.

Naturally, I wonder now whether the laying on of hands in Pentecostal communities does in fact result in a form of kundalini arousal. Could it be that the Baptism of the Holy Spirit is an example of Christian Shaktipat? Swami Muktananda and Gopi Krishna, the two men most responsible for the growing interest in kundalini in the West, have written on several occasions that kundalini energy is what Christians call the Holy Spirit. Is this true? "The Guru and the spiritual energy which he awakens are identical," wrote Swami Muktananda. Could it be that the Holy Spirit is the kundalini energy of the risen Christ?

— Scripture and Kundalini —

The Story of the Fall of Adam and Eve

During the past two years, I have read many articles that discuss the temptation of Adam and Eve by the serpent in relation to kundalini. Most of these writers take the position of Abbé N. de Montfauçon de Villars in *Comte de Gabalis* (cited earlier in this chapter), which holds that the serpent of Eden represented the kundalini force. When Adam and Eve misapplied this energy (sexually?), the energy became directed downward, where it became coiled at the base of the spine. Thereafter, human beings functioned out of the lower three chakras, preoccupied with security, pleasure, and power.

Intriguing though this esoteric view of Scripture may be, it is nonetheless far more important to try to learn what the authors of Scripture intended to say. This has been the burden of twentieth-century Scripture scholarship. Esoteric writers generally assume that all mythological references to serpents are references to kundalini, when, in fact, serpents represented many different energies and experiences in ancient times. Even a cursory glance through such basic references as John McKenzie's *Dictionary of the Bible* and Harper's *Bible Dictionary* will give evidence of the many uses of serpentine symbolism in the literature of the Middle East — many of which have no likeness to kundalini. Sadly, it is not always the practice of writers on the esoteric to do extensive research on their topics.

Traditionally, Christians have viewed the serpent in the Garden as the devil, and I see no reason to change this view. On a psychological level, we can say that this serpent is an extra-Egoic voice that tempts Adam and Eve to disobey God. Although kundalini, too, is an extra-Egoic energy, there is nothing about kundalini in itself which moves one to obey or disobey God. Only the devil and the sin-force that has become incarnate in a disobedient Soul tempts one away from God. To equate kundalini with the serpent in Eden would be, then, to equate kundalini with the devil; this, in my experience, is clearly wrong. It is the Ego that experiences kundalini as demonic, and Adam and Eve represent pre-Egoic humans.

Pentecostal Phenomena

Another place where kundalini experiences may be described in Scripture is in the New Testament accounts of Pentecostal phenomena. Because kundalini energies are often manifest during Pentecostal worship, we might expect to find references to something like kundalini in the New Testament letters of St. Paul. In 1 Corinthians 12, he deals with gifts of the Spirit, some of which (healing, miraculous powers, prophecy) might be attributed to kundalini. Nevertheless, there is in Paul an awareness that the psychic gifts do not of themselves give testimony to the work of the Spirit, for he goes on, in the famous thirteenth chapter, to emphasize the primacy of love over psychic gifts. When listing the fruits of the Spirit in Galatians 5:22–23, Paul mentions "love, joy, peace, patient endurance, kindness, generosity, faith, mildness, and chastity." It is obvious that these qualities may be observed in people who do not have an active kundalini, and that kundalini does not in and of itself bring forth these fruits of the Spirit.

The Story of Simon Magus

Another significant New Testament story can be found in Acts 8:9–24, the story of Simon Magus. We read that a man named Simon was practicing magic and displaying great psychic powers, which influenced many people. When Philip came to town, however, Simon was impressed by the healings and miraculous signs that accompanied the preaching of the Gospel. Simon became a believer, but kept trying to find out how the disciples worked their "magic." When he offered Peter money for this secret, Peter confronted him harshly for his self-centered motives. Simon repented and begged the disciples to pray for him.

What interests me about the case of Simon the magician is that it seems that kundalini powers were at work in Simon before he came to faith in Christ. He saw something of the same happening in the Baptism of the Spirit, but he assumed it could be manipulated by human means. In the end, he was given the message that the Holy Spirit is more interested in the orientation of consciousness than in its psychic powers.

The Saraph Serpents

Perhaps the most intriguing example of a pure experience of kundalini energy can be noted in the Old Testament Book of Numbers 21:4–9. The Jews had been wandering in the desert for many days, and they were complaining about food and drink. Then, "in punishment the Lord sent among the people saraph serpents, which bit the people so that many of them died." I believe it likely that these saraph ("fiery") serpents represented awakened kundalini energies, rather than reptilian serpents, which the people could certainly have avoided.

The people had been wandering in the desert for a long time. This walking in the sun, day after day, must surely have instilled in many an open, nonreflective state of mind. Also, they had been eating the same bland food (manna), which would be favorable to kundalini awakening (a heavier, mixed diet would complexify the physiological processes). Meditation, movement, and diet are three factors mentioned again and again in the literature on kundalini, and all three seem to be favorably present among the Jews in exodus.

When the saraph serpents appeared, they killed those who cursed God. Cursing God is a refusal of the Ego to give up its privileged place in consciousness. To resist awakened kundalini energies in this manner is not only foolhardy, but downright dangerous. We note, too, that those who cursed God were complaining about food and drink, which are first chakra concerns. To be attached to first chakra concerns when kundalini awakens creates maximum resistance to the energy. I have no difficulty believing that there were fatalities as a consequence of this predicament.

The resolution of this dilemma came to Moses from the Lord. "Make a saraph and mount it on a pole, and if any who has been bitten looks at it, he will recover. Moses accordingly made a bronze serpent and mounted it on a pole, and whenever anyone who had been bitten by a serpent looked at the bronze serpent, he recovered."

I am struck by the similarity between vipassana meditation and the above passage. Vipassana is just-looking at one's inner processes in a kind of nonjudgmental, validating attitude. This is the best kind of meditation for allowing kundalini energies to move through the brain. As chapter 1 recounts, I did not begin to experience an improvement in my condition until I changed my attitude toward kundalini from adversarial to welcoming. To look openly upon that which one fears is a courageous and healing thing to do. This is precisely what happens in vipassana and Zen. Perhaps, in similar fashion, the act of looking at the bronze serpent on a pole enabled those inflicted with saraph serpents to let go of their fear toward the serpents. It is this fear and other emotional pains that give kundalini its "bite."

What intrigues me most about this passage is that it is taken up again in the New Testament by Christ, in his conversation with Nicodemus (John 3:14–15).

Just as Moses lifted up the serpent in the desert, so must the Son of Man be lifted up, that all who believe may have eternal life in him.

It is significant that Christ identifies himself and eternal life in some way with the saraph serpents. I am not sure how kundalini ties in here, for the main point seems to be the connection between belief in Christ and his being lifted up, or crucified. As a Catholic who attends Mass in churches where a large crucifix is featured behind the altar, I associate the serpent on the pole with the crucified Christ. To look lovingly upon the crucified Christ can help one to accept the fact of one's eventual death. It is, after all, this fear of death that contributes to the split between the Ego and the Ground. Acceptance of death, then, brings openness to the Ground and its energies, which includes kundalini. This, at least, is how I interpret the story of the saraph serpents and their connection with the crucified Christ. I am aware that other interpretations are also possible — some of which have nothing to do with kundalini. As with so many other areas we have discussed in this book, much more research and dialogue is needed concerning the evidence of kundalini in Scripture.

The Sound Eye (Matt. 6:22–23)

In a famous passage from the Sermon on the Mount, we hear Jesus saying:

The lamp of the body is the eye. It follows that if your eye is sound, your whole body will be filled with light. But if your eye is diseased, your whole body will be all darkness. If then, the light inside you is darkness, what darkness that will be. (Matt. 6:22–23, Jerusalem Bible)

There is much about this passage that sounds like kundalini — especially the reference to inner light and the sound eye. Lee Sannella told me that the original translations referred to the single eye, instead of the sound eye. I checked around and discovered that the King James Version of the Bible did indeed speak of the single eye as a contrast to the evil eye. However, the *Jerome Biblical*

Commentary states that the original Hebrew adjective is obscure, meaning something like simple, single, and sound, in contrast to the envious eye.

At this time, I see no reason to believe that this reference to the single eye in Matthew is the same as the experience of the inner eye or third eye in kundalini transformation. The inner eye is more of a psycho-physiological experience, and Jesus seems to be speaking of a moral attitude.

The Holy Spirit and Fire (Luke 3:16)

It is only in the Gospel of Luke that we hear John the Baptist saying,

> I baptize you with water, but someone is coming, someone who is more powerful than I am, and I am not fit to undo the strap of his sandals; he will baptize you with the Holy Spirit and fire. (Luke 3:16, Jerusalem Bible)

Matthew and Mark mention the Baptism of the Spirit, but eliminate the reference to Baptism by fire.

Most exegeses of this passage state that the terms "Holy Spirit" and "fire" are synonymous. It was common in Old Testament theophanies to refer to God as a fire, and, it is held, this is just another reference to God-as-fire. Other writers state that the reference to fire indicates the process of purification that those living in the Spirit will go through.

I am intrigued, however, by Luke's references to Spirit and fire. In describing the first Baptism of the Spirit, he writes:

> When Pentecost day came round, they had all met in one room, when suddenly they heard what sounded like a powerful wind from heaven, the noise of which filled the entire house in which they were sitting; and something appeared to them that seemed like tongues of fire; these separated and came to rest on the head of each of them. They were all filled with the Holy Spirit and began to speak foreign languages as the Spirit gave them the gift of speech. (Acts 2:1–4)

It is possible that these references to wind and fire might be only symbolic ways of speaking of ineffable experiences. Nevertheless, there is much about this which literally rings true with my own experiences of the Holy Spirit.

More than any other writer in the New Testament, Luke emphasizes the reality of the Baptism of the Spirit. He describes two stages of conversion: the first, a coming to faith in Christ, which is celebrated with Baptism, and the second, the Baptism of the Holy Spirit, conferred by the laying on of hands from the Apostles. Signs of the Baptism of the Spirit are speaking in tongues, prophecy, healing, miracles, and great joy. I have experienced all these in various degrees since my days in Charismatic Renewal, 1973–76, and I can affirm that sensations like wind and fire often accompany the Baptism of the Spirit.

What interests me most, now, is Luke's reference to a Baptism by Fire. Although I have no exegetical basis for proposing that this is a second state of the Baptism of the Spirit, it is here that I find my experiences validated by Scripture. Following my adult conversion and Baptism of the Spirit in 1973, I lived out of a Spirit-centered Ego. Beginning in 1986, however, the transformational process described in this book dismantled the Spirit-centered Ego and led me into a purification process that has been both extremely painful and fruitful. This Baptism of Fire, the kundalini experience, developed out of prayer and Christian living. Therefore, I view my experience of kundalini as a second phase of the Baptism of the Spirit, the purpose of which has been to cleanse my being of emotional pain and bring me to integration at the level of Soul. This Baptism has been a movement of grace; it is nothing that the Ego has accomplished.

What once confused me was that many of the experiences of kundalini I read about did not seem to be related to the Holy Spirit. When I read that many Hindus claimed that kundalini was the Holy Spirit, I became even more confused.

Having read and reflected much on this topic, I am now prepared to say that the kundalini process may or may not give testimony to the work of the Holy Spirit. For those living the life of the Spirit, the kundalini process could be experienced as a deeper Baptism, or purification process. Others may enter the kundalini process as a result of working the disciplines of breathing and posture that release repressed Soul energies into the body. In short, kundalini process is no sure sign of the Spirit and no guarantee for the life of holiness. Dualistic though this conclusion may sound —

separating the Holy Spirit from the kundalini process — I am convinced that it is important that this distinction be made, or else we shall make the mistake of regarding all people with kundalini experiences as sages, prophets, and agents of the Holy Spirit.

The Holy Spirit as the Kundalini Energy of Christ

Finally, and by way of wondering out loud, I think it is worth reflecting on the possibility that the Holy Spirit just might be the kundalini energy of the risen Christ. Developing these reflections fully is beyond the scope of this book, but they could help us to more deeply understand the meaning of the Mystical Body of Christ and the regeneration of the Soul. Christianity has always maintained that the Soul is not-God (even though it is of-God), and that because of sin the Soul has lost its natural experience of God. Christianity also maintains that the Soul is healed through faith in Christ and the restorative action of the Holy Spirit. The energies of the Holy Spirit must, then, be compatible with our human, Soul energies. Since Christ was human, His Soul energies, though more intense than ours, are nevertheless harmonious with ours. In restoring a Soul, He takes it into His own Body, whereafter the Soul lives not by its own created volition, but through participation in the Life of the Body. Thus is the Soul remade in the image of Christ while being fully restored to the fullness of its own created energies.

— *Chapter 6* —

SUMMARY

— What Is Kundalini Energy? —

On an experiential level, kundalini energy is simultaneously pure libido, pure psychic energy, and pure spiritual consciousness.

A theoretical definition of kundalini would be that it is the energy of the Dynamic Ground of Consciousness, which is the undifferentiated energy of the body-Soul union. This definition is similar, in many respects, to the Hindu idea of kundalini as Shakti, the inner (and feminine) power of God.

All bio-energy systems are, ultimately, charged with this energy, for it is the very life force in every person. However, the repressive and defensive mechanisms in Egoic consciousness prevent one from experiencing the full power of kundalini. Consequently, it is rightly said that, for most, kundalini is a dormant energy.

— How Is Kundalini Energy Awakened? —

Kundalini energy in its pure, undifferentiated form is experienced only after the personal and prepersonal dimensions of the unconscious mind have emptied their contents. Of course, kundalini is the energy "pushing" this cleansing process, and so the emptying of the unconscious is itself a "colored" experience of kundalini energy.

It may be said, then, that practices that facilitate the breakdown of Egoic defenses can help to awaken kundalini. The most effective method is a combination of meditation and yogic postures such as those taught in Hatha Yoga. Also effective are laying on of hands in prayer, certain drug experiences, praying in tongues, near-death experiences, certain ritualized sexual practices (Tantric sex), and intensive chanting and/or dancing. If these practices only temporarily puncture the seal of repression between the conscious and unconscious mind, the kundalini energies will erupt until the repressive mechanisms are "repaired." Such an arousal, then, is short-lived in comparison with a full-blown awakening, in which at least part of the repressive seal is permanently ruptured.

— What Is the Significance of a Kundalini Awakening? —

1. Kundalini awakening signals a reversal of the mechanisms of Original Repression, which enabled the Egoic pole to differentiate from its bodily base. If the Ego is balanced and cooperative, a new synthesis can be reached between the conscious "I" and its "Am," or Dynamic Ground. If the Ego is unbalanced, fragmented, and/or uncooperative, kundalini awakening can lead to various psychic disturbances — even permanent insanity, owing to the uneven distribution of energy flowing into the brain. Unbalanced and emotionally colored kundalini awakenings can also overstrain physiological systems, resulting in physical pain, and, in extremely rare cases, death.

2. Kundalini awakening signals a dramatic change in the energy dynamics of the psycho-physiological systems. This change is analogous to adolescence, when the psycho-physiological systems were "wired," as it were, for reproduction. With the awakening of kundalini, something of a reversal of adolescence takes place, with the sexual energy becoming genitally diminished and more diffused throughout the body.

3. Kundalini awakening cleanses the bodily tissues of the physiological roots of emotional pain, allowing the tissues to function more efficiently.

4. As a consequence of the above three factors, a kundalini awakening signals the beginning of the end of the Mental Ego, which maintained itself as a differentiated pole of consciousness through conceptual attachments and emotion-laden defense mechanisms. Kundalini dismantles the defense mechanisms by stripping them of their physiological roots. Thus open to the Dynamic Ground, the Ego stands disoriented and eventually drops its conceptual ties.

5. As the energy of the Dynamic Ground, kundalini awakens one on a level of Soul, which is the True Self experience. This Soul experience is simultaneously one-with-God and not-God.

6. It is written in many places that kundalini is evolutionary energy. This is true to the extent that we accept the likelihood that the expanded states of consciousness brought about in a kundalini awakening are part of our human evolutionary future.

7. In the context of spirituality, it can be seen that a kundalini awakening helps one to bring greater energies and psychic gifts into the service of Love. Kundalini awakening is no guarantee of holiness, however. Free will persists and, with it, the possibility of misusing freedom. Love, too, must continually be chosen.

— What Are the Signs and Symptoms — of a Kundalini Awakening?

Most of the symptoms listed below will be experienced at some time during the kundalini process. Not all will be experienced at once, however (thank God!). Generally, a person who has experienced awakened kundalini will have at least three of these symptoms occurring regularly through the day.

1. Inner vision illuminated when the eyes are closed, especially during times of prayer and meditation. Visual background turning blue, purple, ultraviolet, gold, silver, or white, sometimes forming circular, amoeboid, or tunnel-like patterns.

2. Sensations of heat and/or cold in different parts of the body, especially the shoulders and the top of the head.

3. Tingling sensations in the brain, ears, forehead, spine, and other parts of the body. Feeling like an electrical current is shooting through these places, often snapping or popping through nerves.

4. Sensations of a warm, energized fluid slowly pushing its way around the brain and/or up the spine.

5. Perception of inner sounds — ringing, chirping, buzzing, ringing in the ears.

6. Strong compulsion to be alone and to meditate very deeply.

7. Strong compulsion to close eyes tightly, especially during meditation.

8. Very deep and quiet states of consciousness during meditation; sense of going down into an abyss, or "black hole."

9. Alteration of breathing patterns — sometimes slow and shallow (especially during meditation), short and choppy, or deep and smooth. Growing preference for abdominal breathing.

10. Sensations of electrical energy rippling through the reproductive organs.

11. Sensations of gaseous bubbles arising from the area of the reproductive organs.

12. Compulsion to move facial muscles and bodily limbs in yoga-like postures.

13. Emotional release through weeping and deep sighs.

14. Disorientation in sense of self — not feeling oneself. Sense of "fading," of not really being here.

15. Loss of affective memory; loss of a felt sense of Egoic continuity. "Flattening" of memory.

16. Sense of an inner eye seeing with the two sense eyes. Sense of warmth and strength emanating from the center of the forehead.

17. Inability to stay focused in logical-conceptual consciousness. Inner resistance to conceptualization.

18. Drowsiness when energy is pushing its way into the brain.

19. Pain in the area of the heart and stomach — especially if one has not eaten for a few hours.

— What Are Some Ways to Cope with and Integrate — Awakened Kundalini Energies?

1. Don't panic! Fear only colors the energy darkly. There is nothing to fear if you cooperate with the process (or at least don't frustrate it too much).

2. Find someone to talk to about what is happening to you — preferably someone who knows about kundalini or spiritual growth.

3. Accept the process as a sign of growth. Be grateful for the growth that is taking place within, painful though it may be.

4. Do not work against the process. Pay attention to what hurts, and back off on activities that seem to frustrate the process (e.g., heavy reading, drinking alcohol, using drugs, smoking, immoderate sex, even too much meditation). Learn to "go with the flow."

5. Keep your intent of consciousness focused on BEING HERE NOW IN LOVE.

6. Let the various states of consciousness produced by kundalini come and go. Experience and explore them, but do not attach to them. The True Self is not to be found in any particular state of consciousness.

7. Surrender yourself into the care of Christ, Whose Spirit is capable of guiding your kundalini energies toward a wholesome integration. Trust that a Higher Guidance is at work in the process. Ask for this Guidance when confused; listen for the answers.

8. Accept the pains that come and willingly cooperate with asanas and compulsions to meditate. These all pass away in time.

9. Practice yogic asanas for at least fifteen minutes a day to help facilitate the movement of the energy. Also consider using Tai

Chi, massage, and/or movement therapies, especially when the energy seems to be blocked.

10. Learn to breathe abdominally.

11. Practice the mahabandha lock under the supervision of an experienced guide. Tuck the chin into the chest, drawing the navel inward and upward during exhalation while gently contracting the anal sphincter and perineal muscles. Keeping the chin tucked in, relax the muscles during inhalation drawing the navel outward to pull the diaphragm downward. Gently repeat this pattern of contracting and relaxing muscles while exhaling and inhaling deeply, attaching a spiritually focused mantra (e.g., "Come, Lord") to the breathing pattern.

12. Eat a balanced and nutritious diet, avoiding red meat, eggs, spicy foods, alcohol, coffee, and empty calorie sweets. Eat more fruit, vegetables, brown rice, grains, nutritious pastries, cheese, milk, yogurt, tofu, and nuts. These healthy foods probably do play a vital role in producing maximum nutrition and minimum pollution to a body undergoing physiological changes.

13. During times of strong energy upheavals, keep food in the stomach. A small snack such as bread and butter every three hours will help to minimize burning sensations in the stomach.

14. Avoid all forms of willful, competitive activities that generate fear and anger, for these will contaminate the energy with painful emotions.

15. Learn to deal with feelings as they arise through proper communication skills.

16. Males should be especially careful about sexual expression. Although the research on kundalini and sexuality is only in its infancy, the experiences of many (the author included) point up a definite relationship between kundalini energy and sexual energy. Genital sexuality should not be divorced from love, or else one's spiritual energy and physiological responsiveness will be lowered.

17. Creative outlets of expression help to ground the energy. This was a turning point in Gopi Krishna's experience of kundalini, and many others have noted the same. Activities such as dance, song, art, poetry, sculpture, gardening, and even long, quiet walks are helpful.

18. When you don't know what to do to cooperate with the process, it is better to do less than too much. For example, it is better to cut back on meditation than to meditate too much. It is easier to awaken a sleeping serpent than to tame an angry one.

19. Above all, you should be careful about Egoic inflation, especially in the early stages. In certain states of consciousness, you may experience profound psychic gifts and feel like a great spiritual genius. You are still human, however. Even though it is not commonly observed, thousands of people throughout history have gone through this process. It's just a part of our human development — that's all!

20. Get a good night's sleep. If the ears hurt, sleep on your side with the ear hurting most (probably the right ear) downward.

21. If symptoms become too uncomfortably strong and painful, suspend meditation, eat more food, and get more exercise. Gradually resume meditation when uncomfortable symptoms have subsided. If this does not help, seek professional guidance.

POSTSCRIPT

My husband, Phil, has asked me to write about my thoughts and perceptions of what has been going on with him these past four years. I do so quite willingly. He has always shared his spiritual experiences with me, even before our marriage. Our relationship began in Christian community and has been rooted in our Catholic faith even as we individually struggled to let go of various attachments and fears.

When he told me a few years ago about seeing lights in his head (which he later called mandalas), buzzings in the ears, crying for hours at night, energy fizzing from the top of his head, the "crab" in his brain, the pressure inside his ears, I found it all very strange. I did not find *him* strange, however. He was becoming more humble, more sensitive, less defensive and sarcastic. He continued his work and his share of the housework and childcare. As for the increase in prayer time... well, I always knew he needed time for prayer. Sometimes I felt a little sorry for him, having to go through these crazy-sounding things. Sometimes, too, I was a little awed, wondering whom I was married to! But my understanding, which I shared with him and with our support group, was not that he needed medical attention. Rather, I perceived this process as the way God chose to break through Phil's strong intellectualism. He was always a "head" person. In the new prayer experiences which forced him to just "be" — no words, no writing, no thinking — it seemed he was being "rounded out" by God. Since we knew of no other person experiencing anything similar, I figured God must be working with him in a *very individualized* manner!

Discovering that all these strange experiences were called kundalini and were well known in certain forms of yoga was especially reassuring for him. I was glad he had comrades, of a sort. All I could offer was to be a listener who reassured him that I did not think he was crazy. However, the only part that had been familiar to me were the "grimaces" he'd refer to; those I recognized from Hatha Yoga (I was one who frequently did yoga stretches for fitness only), and those grimaces I thought were intended to give strength and flexibility to his facial and neck muscles.

As for myself, I do not expect to experience this kundalini process in the way that Phil has experienced it. We are different in our primary Jungian functions — his being introverted intuition, mine extraverted feeling. Thus, our Shadow experiences are different. We've also talked about gender being a factor. Phil surmises that for women in general, the unfolding of the impersonal feminine power is not such a shock to the system as for men. In any case, my spiritual journey to wholeness is presently different from his. Comparisons of better or worse are not appropriate here. God, Who knows us better than we know ourselves, leads us on the journey. We follow with trust.

LISA BELLECCI-ST. ROMAIN

AFTERWORD

The spontaneous awakening of kundalini-like energies that this book recounts has a significance that goes far beyond the importance it has in the personal life of Philip St. Romain. It is certainly fascinating to be allowed a glimpse into what it is like to suddenly encounter the ancient serpent power, or kundalini, that played so important a role in the religious life of ancient India. But since the author is at once a practicing Catholic devoted to the life of prayer and the recipient of experiences described by the sages of India, he has become, unwittingly, a laboratory in which we can see in microcosm some of the most crucial questions that face Christianity today.

Up until recently Christians have suffered from a mixture of cultural and religious superiority and defensiveness that have restricted their relationship with other religions and the secular world, as well. After the Second Vatican Council all this began to change rapidly. The separations of the past gave way to a growing enthusiasm to find what Christians had in common with Hindus and Zen Buddhists, Jungian psychologists and cosmologists, and these dialogues will have an important impact on the shape of the Church of the future.

But now that these discussions are beginning to mature, the first signs are appearing that this enthusiasm for convergence might be too facile. Is Buddhist enlightenment really the same as the mystical experience of Christians? Is Jung's process of individuation to be identified with prayer? Or must we face the fact that a fully mature dialogue must carefully distinguish differences, not in order to go back to the old separations, but to go forward to a higher and deeper unity?

This is why experiences like that of Philip St. Romain are so important. As a man trained in biology he has to ask how kundalini relates to anatomy and physiology. As a psychotherapist he is compelled to frame a psychological explanation drawing on the findings of depth psychology. And as a Christian he has to grapple with the difficult issue of how to relate his experiences of prayer with the awakening of a new kind of consciousness through kundalini. It is the men and women who experience from within both Hinduism and Christianity or Buddhism and Christianity, or Jungian psychology and Christianity, or modern physics and Christianity, and struggle to be faithful to each reality, in the face of the temptation to give way to hasty identifications, that will lead the way to the creation of a true global culture. The value of Philip St. Romain's book should not be sought first of all in the interesting hypotheses he advances in his attempt to integrate the experience of kundalini with the other aspects of his life; rather it resides in the simple but remarkable fact that he now lives in two worlds that he has to struggle to bring together, not only for his own sake, but for all of us.

JAMES ARRAJ

ANNOTATED BIBLIOGRAPHY

Most of the works listed below have something important to say about kundalini. Those that do not are included because they have been important to me in clarifying the meaning of Christian and Eastern mysticism.

Arraj, James. *St. John of the Cross and Dr. C. G. Jung*. Chiloquin, OR: Inner Growth Books, 1986.
    A very well researched discussion of similarities and differences between Jungian psychology and the mysticism of St. John of the Cross. Includes important distinctions between acquired and passive contemplation.

————. *God, Zen, and the Intuition of Being*. Chiloquin, OR: Inner Growth Books, 1988.
    Explores similarities and differences between Zen and Christian contemplation. Also discusses relevance of Thomistic theology to Zen and contemplation.

Bhajan, Yogi. *Kundalini: Meditation Manual for Intermediate Students*. Los Angeles: Kundalini Research Institute, 1975.
    A workbook for students of Kundalini Yoga. It was from this book that I learned the importance of the neck-lock position.

Da Free John. *Easy Death*. Clearlake, CA: Dawn Horse Press, 1983.
    Although the primary focus of this book is on death and dying, there are several essays on meditation and spirituality. It was here that I found a comprehensive discussion of the colors of the Cosmic Mandala, which are perceived during kundalini awakening. Most significantly, too, the author makes a firm distinction between a loving spirituality centered in the heart and kundalini experiences.

Dass, Ram. *The Only Dance There Is*. Garden City, NY: Anchor/Doubleday, 1973.

A collection of talks given before the Menninger Foundation and Spring Grove Hospital. Includes popular, New Age attitudes concerning chakras and consciousness development, along with a few vague references to kundalini energy.

Eliade, Mircea. *Yoga: Immortality and Freedom*. Princeton, NJ: Bollingen Foundation, Inc., 1969.

A straightforward but rather technical discussion of the beliefs and practices of yoga. Includes extensive discussions on kundalini, but is rather hard reading because of his usage of Sanskrit terms, which are not always well-defined.

Groeschel, Benedict. *Spiritual Passages: The Psychology of Spiritual Development*. New York: Crossroad, 1988.

Discusses the relationships between psychology, spirituality, and theology. The traditional stages of Christian growth — purgative, illuminative, and unitive — are described. Despite this, the author seems to consider unitive experiences a quite rare phenomenon.

Groothuis, Douglas R. *Unmasking the New Age*. Madison, WI: Inter-Varsity Press, 1986.

Despite its somewhat fundamentalist tendencies, this book identifies many differences between Christian and Eastern spirituality and theology. On page 68, the author encourages readers to steer clear of Hatha Yoga because it may awaken kundalini energy; he lists only the possible negative effects of kundalini, but not the positive.

St. John of the Cross. *Dark Night of the Soul*. E. Allison Peers, ed. Garden City, NY: Doubleday, 1959.

A classic in Catholic contemplative literature. Includes many penetrating psychological, spiritual, and theological insights. No references to kundalini are made, but the Dark Nights he describes are very similar to those that accompany kundalini activity.

Kester, Nicola. "Kundalini: The Serpent Power Comes to the West," in *Common Boundary*, July/August 1989, pp. 18–23.

A short review of the current status of kundalini research, featuring interviews with several noted authorities on kundalini.

Keyes, Ken, Jr. *Handbook to Higher Consciousness*. Berkeley, CA: Living Love Center, 1975.

A very popular book among New Age enthusiasts. His seven centers of consciousness are obviously based on the chakra system, but the disciplines he encourages are much simpler than those described

141

in Kundalini Yoga. There is, however, nothing about kundalini energy in this book.

Krishna, Gopi. *Kundalini for the New Age*. Gene Kieffer, ed. New York: Bantam Books, 1988.
A collection of talks and essays delivered on various occasions by Gopi Krishna, the most popular modern writer on kundalini energy. Includes many helpful speculations on the nature and purpose of kundalini energy from the view point of science, psychology, mysticism, and evolution.

———. *Kundalini: The Evolutionary Energy in Man*. Boston: Shambhala Publishing, 1985.
The autobiography of Gopi Krishna, including his account of the awakening of kundalini energy, his struggles to integrate this force, and the astonishing gifts that come to him as a result of this transformation.

Merton, Thomas. *Zen and the Birds of Appetite*. New York: New Directions, 1968.
It is obvious that Merton's primary love in the East was Zen, for he wrote little about Hinduism and kundalini. Even so, this book is helpful for its discussions of the similarities and differences between Eastern and Christian mysticism.

May, Gerald, M.D. *Will and Spirit*. New York: Harper & Row, 1982.
One of the best books on psychology, spirituality, and mysticism that I have ever read! The author is familiar with Eastern and Western mysticism and offers many discussions on the similarities and differences between the two. He also mentions kundalini energy in several places, but only in reference to yoga and the transformation of energy.

Muktananda, Swami. *Kundalini: The Secret of Life*. South Fallsburg, NY: SYDA Foundation, 1979.
A straightforward, easy-to-read discussion of kundalini energy and Siddha Yoga. Includes accounts of how kundalini is awakened, signs of its presence, and the transformations that take place because of its activity.

Radha, Swami Sivananda. *Kundalini Yoga for the West*. Boston: Shambhala Publishing, 1985.
A comprehensive discussion of the meaning and disciplines of Kundalini Yoga, written with the Western psyche in mind. I found her appendix on the problems encountered when kundalini awakens spontaneously to be very helpful.

Roberts, Bernadette. *The Experience of No-Self*. Boston: Shambhala Publishing, 1984.

————. *The Path to No-Self*. Boston: Shambhala Publishing, 1985.
These two books by Bernadette Roberts helped me to be open to possibilities for growth that I had not dreamed of before. She describes her experiences with contemplation and how eventually her I-Thou relationship with God fell away, leaving her with what she describes as pure subjectivity. She also describes many phenomena accompanying this transformation that clearly attest to the activity of an awakened kundalini (see p. 49 of *The Experience* and Phase VI of *Path*). Although her psychological terminology is highly idiosyncratic and her knowledge of Eastern religions is weak, she is well worth reading.

Royo, Antonio, O.P., and Jordan Aumann, O.P. *The Theology of Christian Perfection*. Dubuque: Priory Press, 1962.
Formerly a standard reference for Catholic religious, this book is now considered outdated in its traditional approach to spiritual growth. I find it very helpful, however. The section on extraordinary mystical phenomena includes what I believe to be very clear references to kundalini activity, although it is not labeled as such.

St. Romain, Philip. *Pathways to Serenity*. Liguori, MO: Liguori Publications, 1988.
A description of the framework and spiritual disciplines that have supported my own journey in faith.

————. *Lessons in Loving*. Liguori, MO: Liguori Publications, 1988.
A discussion of relationship skills. Includes worksheets and journal exercises.

Sannella, Lee, M.D. *The Kundalini Experience*. Lower Lake, CA: Integral Publishing, 1987.
This is the best book I have found for understanding the kundalini process from a scientific viewpoint. Dr. Sannella approaches the topic as an objective researcher who nonetheless respects the spiritual dimension of this energy.

Silburn, Lilian. *Kundalini: Energy of the Depths*. Albany, NY: SUNY Press, 1988.
A discussion of the meaning of many ancient texts on kundalini, most of which deal with Tantric sexual practices. Not easy reading for those unfamiliar with Hindu terminology.

Vishnu-devananda, Swami. *The Complete Illustrated Book of Yoga*. New York: Julian Press, Inc., 1988.

This book is what is says: complete and illustrated. It covers topics ranging from metaphysics, diet, and psychology, and includes illustrations of many asanas (yoga postures). The discussions on kundalini energy are most helpful.

Washburn, Michael. *The Ego and the Dynamic Ground*. Albany, NY: SUNY Press, 1988.

I found this book most helpful for situating the kundalini process in a developmental framework. The author's discussion of kundalini as the energy of the Dynamic Ground greatly influenced my own thinking. I strongly recommend this book to anyone interested in transpersonal psychology.